Black On A Background Of White

A Chronicle of Afro-Americans' Involvement in America's Last Frontier, Alaska

by
Everett Louis Overstreet

Alaska Black Caucus

PUBLISHED BY
ALASKA BLACK CAUCUS

DISTRIBUTED BY
THAT NEW PUBLISHING CO.
1525 EIELSON ST.
FAIRBANKS, AK 99701

MANUFACTURED IN THE UNITED STATES OF AMERICA

LIBRARY OF CONGRESS #87-72928

ISBN 0-918270-20-0

Contents

In Dedication to:

The Overstreets, Myrtha, Rudy, JoAnn, Lorie, Piper, my nieces, Toni, Lyne, Terri, Jeanni, Kathi, and Vickki, nephew, Ryan, godsons, LeRoy, and Kenny, Percy and Ann Gregory, Jimmie James......."Ebbie" and "Lump Lump" wherever you may be.

Special Thanks To:

The aunts and uncles and family friends that provided needed guidance during my formative years, Ann Powell and Norman Johnson who have had the most influence on my educational outlook, my mentors Parren Mitchell, Tony Brown, Walter Fauntroy, Earl Graves, Mickey Leland, Troy James, "My leader", Calvin Rolark, and Grace Likeness who typed the manuscript for this book.

FOREWORD:

As ways for organizing and presenting the material contained in this book were considered, it was the most comfortable for me to parallel what the contributions others have made to my growth as an individual with that which has been the growth of a black presence in Alaska.

While attending the all black elementary school, R. B. Hayes in Cleveland, Ohio, I'm sure classmates, Roosevelt Thurman and Janice Lindsay, and I did not fully appreciate our teachers. However, it is now clear that a debt of gratitude is owed to these individuals that provided us with the educational, emotional, and psychological reinforcements necessary to adapt to our bicultural existence in America.

I still chuckle over how Lana Wimbs and I used to sit on our front porches and, at best, only gain a vicarious appreciation for the work ethic values that were being instilled in my close friend, Tommie "Emmo" Rowell by his parents.

My partners from East Tech High, Charles "Big Chuck" Bremer, and Bob "Boomer" Brown and I have talked about and long ago reached the conclusion that the reason Joe Howell and other teachers "stayed on our cases" was to prepare us to be able to combat the stress in our lives that confronting the inequities that exist in America was going to induce.

A lot of these earlier teachings, which clearly supported the need to remain vigilant, to my later chagrin, were temporarily lost when I went off to attend an integrated college and incorrectly assumed the lack of structure, I perceived, equated to the lack of a need for self discipline, much less needing to maintain a vigil. Fred "Hamp the Lamp" Hamilton, Huey Ball, Benson Penick, Joe Peters, Glenn Hill, Al Bogan, Dave Pearson, Frances Holly, Leon Hogg, Ricky Jenkins, Jeannie Hairston, and Cleve Bryant and I thought, at the time, life was always going to be like the times at "Fun U." When Sanford "Pee Wee" Rivers, our buddy from another school, received a signing bonus to try out for pro football, this event served to reinforce the perception that life was going to be all wine and roses, and that the values I had learned, accepted and attempted to practice while growing up would no longer be needed.

Thankfully not all the people that I have been associated with over the years have suffered with my affliction of a lack of vision.

Many were and remain aware of the fact that, while not the majority, too many people in power are intent on having America's history also be her future. They want us to despair over the fact that history reveals that the content of one's character, is no match for the color of another person's skin, and that ability as well as gender can not beat bigotry.

However, the younger generation like the students who attended Carnegie Mellon University in the early seventies, Tanya Allmond, Linda Arnold, Leonard Bell, Debra Watkins, Tony Brown, "Diablo" Scott, Tony

Maddox and Reggie Govan, who will be assuming leadership positions within the next decade, are blessed with a vision of a different future for America.

Similarly, persons who are carrying the banner of leadership up here in Alaska like Pat Berkley, Bettye Davis, and Bill Sykes, as well as those who have paid their dues like Sterling Taylor, and Fred Johnson, not to mention those on the way up, Rex Butler, Winston Henderson, and Henry Lancaster have a vision and are working for a change that is imminent.

They clearly see that character will come back in the late rounds of the match to score a knockout over the color of a person's skin as a future consideration for advancement, and that ability will come on and overtake and beat bigotry at the tape to win the gold medal of equality for all Americans

Everett Louis Overstreet
Anchorage, Alaska
November, 1987

INTRODUCTION

Alaska's history, first as a territory purchased from Russia, and much later as a state, totals less than 120 years.

Up until the start of World War II, less than 75,000 people inhabited a land mass of 365 million acres.

While there has been a documented presence of Afro-Americans in Alaska since 1870, this presence has gone largely unreported. This omission serves as the basis for the discussion herein presented.

The discussion is not presented as a strict historical accounting, but is proffered as a journal of individuals and events. It is hoped the work will have anecdotic appeal to the pleasure reader, serve as a primer for students, and form the basis from which research, by professionals, of a more definitive and substantive nature may embark.

Given that the migration of blacks to Alaska did not occur in significant numbers until the decade of the forties, this work has benefited from the fact that there currently exists a first-hand oral history that most likely will not be in evidence by the turn of the century. To these pioneer Alaskans who have graciously shared their remembrances, a debt of gratitude is owed.

CHAPTER I
EARLY YEARS, THE ADVENTURERS

The widely publicized, and at the time ridiculed purchase of Alaska[1] by the United States from Russia in 1867 was characterized as "Seward's Folly". The saying was a reference to William Seward, who as Secretary of State arranged the purchase of Alaska for the magnificent sum, at the time, of $7,200,000. Ridicule aside, when viewed in retrospect, the United States was able to acquire the most energy rich territory in the Americas for approximately two cents an acre.

Historical accounts would seem to support the popular belief that the colonization of Alaska was accomplished without the brutality that was associated with westward expansion in the contiguous states in the early 19th century.

Some historians account for this phenomenon with socio-political references to the docile nature of the Native inhabitants and the exhibition of more benign attitudes by the colonists than those exhibited earlier in our nation's history.

However, the truth is more related to the fact that a sparse Native population base which was separated by language differences, climatic and geographical extremes, did not pose a real or imagined threat to the colonists. Thus, humane attitudes could be benignly exhibited rather than those of a more base nature.

Early census data[2] gives a hint as to the type of social behavior that was in evidence in Alaska's early territorial days. The percentage of males to females in the Native population was 51 percent males to 49 percent females. Whereas, the percentage totals for the other population groups were 95 percent males to 5 percent females. Discounting for the fact that a few of the nearly 8,000 non-native population was comprised of families, this still left an enormous disparity between the number of males (7,400) and females (400).

Predictably, a number of inter-racial relationships evolved during this period in Alaska's history. Just as predictably, a number of ladies were available for a "good time". These ladies who were possessed with a giving nature and sense of community spirit are a colorful part of the folklore that exists in the state.

At the time Alaska was purchased by the United States, there existed only one settlement that could be considered a town. The remaining settlements were comprised of trading posts and Native villages.

The town of Sitka, Alaska was occupied by the Army in 1868 which had been assigned the responsibility of governing Alaska. The civilian population count of Sitka that was recorded by the Army in 1870 totaled 1,542 people. The Native population totaled 1,251 persons and the non-Native population was recorded at 391 persons. Six blacks were recorded in the count of 391 people. Three of the six were from the Caribbean Islands.

Of the remaining three blacks, two were a married couple who worked on the Navy ship Cyane and the other was a servant named Mary who came to Alaska with an Army doctor and his family. Their last name was Fitzgerald. Mrs. Fitzgerald's letters to friends alleged that Mary was a person who enjoyed the company of the soldiers stationed in Sitka. Mrs. Fitzgerald also indicated that she had to fire Mary because Mary had contacted a social disease. Mary left Alaska for Portland, Oregon two years after her arrival.

Michael Healy sailed Alaskan waters first as an officer and later as Captain of several revenue cutters[3] from 1880 to the middle of the first decade of the 20th century. Ships he commanded included the Bear (1886-1896), Mc Culluck (1900), and the Thelis (1902, 1903).

Records of the day also reveal black men served on vessels engaged in whaling before the turn of the century.

Blacks were among the thousands of people who flocked to the Klondike gold fields in 1896. A black woman, Bessie Couture ran a restaurant in Skagway called the "Black and White Restaurant".

St. John Atherton, a former slave from Georgia, recovered $30,000 worth of gold in the Klondike in 1897 and left the state.

In the spring of 1898, Company L, 24th Infantry, U. S. Army arrived at Dyea to maintain order among the people bound for the Klondike gold fields. The black soldiers were commanded by a white officer, Captain Henry Hovey. The company departed Alaska in May of 1902.

As a historical note, the 24th Infantry, along with the 25th, and the 9th and 10th Calvary were established by legislation enacted in 1866 and 1869. The 1866 Act reorganized the Army into ten calvary regiments and 45 infantry regiments. Two calvary and

Proctecting Mining Claim, Circa 1900

Mining For Gold, Circa 1900

Prizefighter, Black Prince, waiting on tables at the "Social Club".

four infantry regiments had black enlisted personnel. The 1869 Act reduced the number of infantry units and consolidated the black 38th and 41st regiments into the 24th Infantry.

Historian, Blanche McSmith[4], in a newspaper article[5] discussed the lifestyles of several early arrivals to Alaska.

Black Prince was a prizefighter during gold rush days. However, because very few people were willing to fight him, he wound up serving as a bouncer and waiter in a saloon in Dawson called the Monte Carlo Club.

William Waddington arrived in Alaska in 1894. He was recalled as a flashy dresser and a person with outspoken and controversial views. Records indicate that in 1917 he was arrested for treason for passing out Socialist Party pamphlets. He was fined $75 for his actions. He died in 1938.

While black men and women of the time came to Alaska in search of gold, others like their majority counterparts referenced earlier, found it easier to engage in the oldest profession. "Black Kitty in Circle City, and "Black Alice" in Nome were well known "good timers" of the day. Of the 168 blacks reported in the 1900 Alaskan Census, 93 lived in Skagway.

After the gold rush, a number of blacks remained in Alaska. Mattie "Tootsie" Crosby opened a restaurant and bath house at Flat, Alaska in the Iditarod mining district in 1911. She operated the restaurant until she entered the Pioneer House in Sitka in 1962. She died in 1972.

In 1929 Lulu Swanson arrived in Anchorage and opened a hotel. As legend would have it a variety of services, in keeping with the Alaskan tradition, were available at the hotel. By the early 1950's she had become one of the largest land holders in Anchorage.

John Cleveland in 1928 was the first black to enroll at the Alaska Agricultural College and School of

Mines[6]. now named the University of Alaska, Fairbanks.

1. Corruption of a Native (Aleut) word roughly translated to mean "Great Land".
2. U. S. Census of Alaska, 1890.
3. Revenue Cutters were responsible for enforcing maritime laws, assisting ships in need, and stopping at coastal villages to maintain law and order.
4. First black to serve in State of Alaska's Legislature.
5. Anchorage Times, February 20, 1982 edition, Blacks In The Shadow of Alaska's History.
6. The college was opened in 1922.

CHAPTER II
GROWTH YEARS, SETTLING THE LAST FRONTIER

While growth in Alaska's population has been relatively steady, since the first census data was compiled in 1890, much of this growth has taken place since the beginning of World War II.

In the first 50 years of census gathering (1890-1940) Alaska's population experienced a 125 percent increase (32,052 to 72,524).

During this period of time there was only a minimal increase in the permanent black population (112 to 141). The recorded black population remained less than one half of one percent throughout this period of time.

In the last 40 years of census taking (1940-1980) the state's population grew by 450 percent (72,524 to 401,851).[1]

During this same period of time the black population increased by nearly a hundredfold (141 to 13,748).

Today, blacks comprise the largest minority group in both of Alaska's largest cities.[2]

TABLE I
CENSUS DATA
ALASKAN POPULATION
1890 -1980

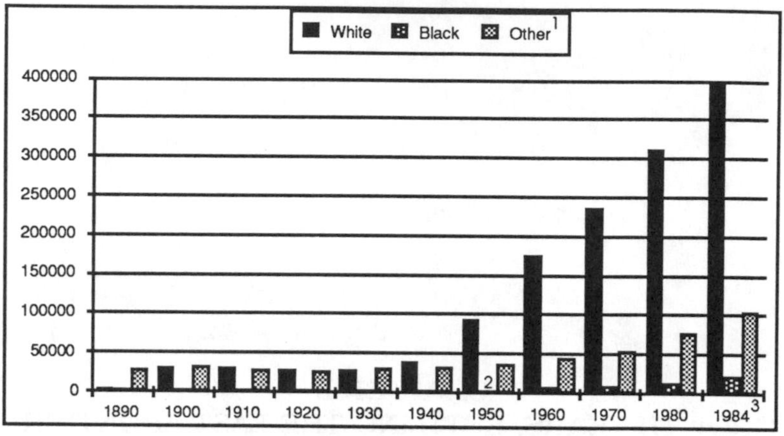

CENSUS DATA
ALASKAN POPULATION
1890 -1980
POPULATION BY PERCENTAGE

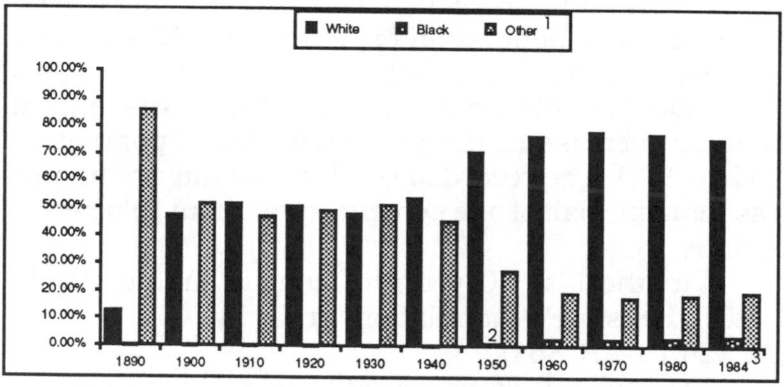

1. Includes Natives, Indians, Hispanic and Asian Americans.
2. 1950 Census count included in this total Black, Chinese, Japanese and Filippinos.
3. Estimate completed by the State for Alaska Department of Labor.

TABLE II
ALASKA'S TWO LARGEST CITIES
POPULATION (TOTAL BLACK)

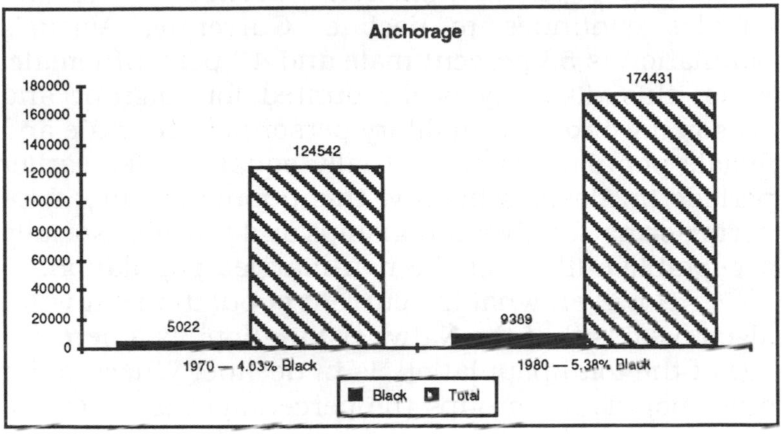

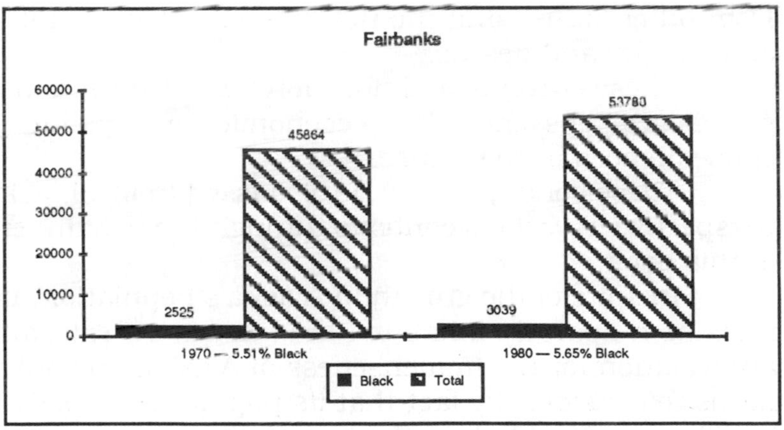

The population disparity between males and females referenced in Chapter I has all but been eliminated. Successive census data reveal that the percentage population difference between males and females continues to decline. Currently, Alaska's population is 53 percent male and 47 percent female. When this disparity is discounted for migrant and seasonal workers, or military personnel, the male and female populations are virtually equal. Unlike earlier periods in Alaska's history, this population mix supports normal family relationships and provides socially acceptable outlets for the non-married population.

However, what the current population statistics also reveal is that the Native population, as a percentage of the total population, is in decline. Whereas, for other population groups the percentages are increasing.

This phenomenon is attributable to the fact the Native population must depend solely on in-state growth as a function of the net difference between births and deaths. Whereas, other population groups are increasing their numbers both through migration from other states, and the net difference between in-state births and deaths.

These current conditions foretell of tremendous sociological, psychological, economic and political consequences in the future.

These conditions will be discussed from a black perspective in various contexts through the remainder of this book.

In spite of the growth in Alaska's population, it remains a sparsely inhabited land mass. To gain an appreciation for the immenseness of Alaska, one only needs to consider the fact that its population density, is still considerably less than one person per square mile. As a comparison, California, our nation's most populous state, has a population density of one hundred sixty one persons per square mile.

As discussed in Chapter I, up until the late thirties much of Alaska's population was comprised of people indigenous to the region who depended on a subsistence lifestyle for their survival, with a liberal sprinkling of people from the "Lower 48"[3] in search of adventure and a future, and those trying to escape a past.

Today the majority of Alaska's population is comprised of first and second generation migrants from the contiguous states who perform services in exchange for wages.

The early revenue producing industries of fishing, mining, and trapping, while still in existence, have been supplanted in importance by other industries. The oil industry, capital construction, military support activities, and tourism are the state's new sources of revenue generation.[4] However, it is government (federal, state and municipal) that is the largest single employer.[5]

Taxation of the oil industry provides upwards of 85 percent of the revenue that funds the state's operating and capital budgets.

Correspondingly, the construction industry in Alaska has been very active for much of the past decade. In a number of instances these activities have led to over built conditions in urban areas, and public capital projects in rural areas that are under utilized with the maintenance of these facilities having a negative impact on the state's annual operating budgets.

Since the advent of World War II, there has been an ongoing military build-up in Alaska. The military presence in Alaska has for many years provided an economic stimulus to the state's economy.

Military spending is projected to top one-half billion dollars in 1987.

Currently, military strategists are pushing to

TABLE III
1985 Annual Employment by Industry

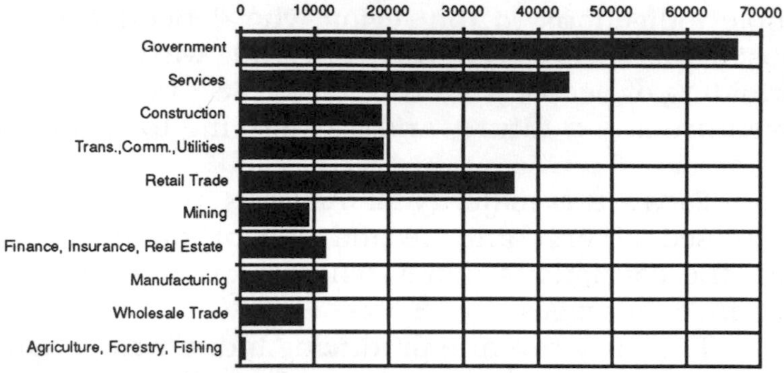

Source: State of Alaska, Department of Labor.

have land based nuclear weapons deployed in Alaska. The citizens, in an advisory vote in October, 1986 by a substantial majority, were opposed to such deployment.

Tourism has been gaining in importance each year as a source of revenue. Since the late seventies more people visit Alaska annually than the number of people who permanently reside in the state. In 1986 nearly three quarters of a million people visited Alaska. The state's estimated total population at the end of 1986 was just over a half million people.

The 1940 census recorded 141 black people residing in Alaska.

Fortunately there still exists an oral history of what lifestyles have been like for the past fifty years and is covered in additional detail in other chapters. To the persons who have provided much of the information, herein contained, attempts have been made to identify a number of these individuals.

Civilian construction work opportunities in support of seasonal private projects, and year round military projects were the first magnets attracting a number of blacks to Alaska. Later integration of the armed forces gave blacks an opportunity to experience Alaska.

There were a number of blacks employed in the construction of Elmendorf and Ft. Richardson Military Bases outside of Anchorage at the start and during World War II. The bases provided employment for Mr. Zelmer Lawrence, who is the surviving black with the longest continuous length of residency in the state. He arrived in Cordova, Alaska in 1938. He was married a short time later to his sweetheart from Seattle, Washington. Mrs. Lawrence gave up a promising show business career to join the man she loved in Alaska. She remained in Alaska up until the time of her death in 1974. They moved to Anchorage in 1940, after the copper mining activity petered out in Cordova.

Mr. Lawrence went to work at Elmendorf in the winter of 1942 as a carpenter supervisor. In what had to be somewhat precedent setting for the day, he supervised a military unit of Florida National Guardsmen. In recalling the times, he spoke more of the camaraderie that existed between them than any difficulty that might have been associated with a northern non-military black, giving orders to southern military whites. He recalled, with fondness, the fact the troops worked hard and engaged in the only social outlet of the time, drinking. This condition often resulted in Mr. Lawrence having to cover for the troops, who were sleeping off hangovers, with their officers. The wages, Mr. Lawrence and other civilians earned, were between $.95 - $1.25 an hour.

"When I arrived in Alaska in 1942, there were only thirteen colored people living in Fairbanks and one public bath house," recalls forty five year Alaskan resident, Jo Elizabeth Porter. "After holding down a variety of jobs, I settled into a 26 year career with the U. S. Postal Service." Since retiring in the mid-seventies, she has been active in a host of volunteer organizations.

As blacks migrated to Alaska in ever increasing numbers in the forties and fifties, the cities of Anchorage and Fairbanks served as primary locations for settlement.

The obstacles to overcome at the time were climatic extremes, limited accommodations, and marginal conveniences.

In Fairbanks, the summer temperatures can rise above 90° and in the winter as low as -60° below zero. In Anchorage, because of the moderating effect of the mountains and the ocean, the temperature variance is not nearly as extreme, ranging from a high of 80° in the summer to near zero in the winter.

The basis for blacks migrating to Alaska were similar to that which prompted blacks to migrate from the rural south to the urban north in the twenties and thirties. The people were in search of a better life, translated to mean good paying jobs. Many of the new arrivals were forced to stay with relatives or friends. Well into the fifties the Polar Hotel located on 5th Avenue near Cordova Street was the only public facility willing to provide accommodations for blacks, in Anchorage.

In the early fifties there was only one main street paved in Anchorage (4th Avenue). The area where blacks were concentrated was called Eastchester Flats[6] Sam and Catherine LeViege, typical of the couples arriving in Anchorage at the time, recalled the fact that housing in this area was served by community toilets and wells. This area was served by one black food store (Adams Grocery) and several night spots, which are discussed in Chapter IV.

Conditions in this area did not measurably

Univetures Building Anchorage, Alaska

Ribbin Cutting Ceremonies, June 20, 1985
(l to r) Congressman Mickey Leland,
M. Grant, S. LeViege, C. Leviege,
D. LeViege, L. LeViege & C. Williams.

improve until the area was designated for urban renewal in the 60's. Residential lots in this area that were selling for $500 in 1950, were assessed in 1986 by the Municipality of Anchorage at $70,000 a lot.

Sam and Catherine LeViege first arrived in Anchorage on April 1, 1952. After a number of years of working in a variety of construction and service jobs they bought a small painting company. By the time they retired in 1986, Northwest Painting Company had grown into one of the most successful painting companies in Alaska. Also, the LeViege family were the first blacks to complete a commercial development valued in excess of a million dollars. The Univentures Building located at 13th and Gambell, upon completion in 1985, was valued at 2.3 million dollars.

In Fairbanks, long time Fairbanks Branch, NAACP President, J. P. Jones, owns a commercial structure that houses a barber shop, arcade, ice house business, and a grocery store. His store has to have one of the all time great names for a convenience grocery store, "Pick and Git".

His advocacy efforts on behalf of the black community are legendary. His public debate with Governor Jay Hammond over how the State Human Rights Commission was being run lead to his dismissal as a commissioner.

After a number of well publicized incidents of housing discrimination in the early sixties, and the establishment of the State's Human Rights Commission[7], housing became available to blacks throughout Anchorage. By the mid seventies residential housing problems had all but been eliminated, and housing patterns today are more readily identifiable with income levels, than race.

The areas where there exists the largest concentration of blacks in the 1980's are the Fairview and Mountain View neighborhoods.

However, even in these areas, blacks do not comprise the largest percentage of residents.

Blacks living in Alaska in the late forties and throughout the fifties, by the accounts of long time Alaskans, could generally be described as members and family of the military, persons and their families who had craft skills related to construction, and people in the personal service areas (beauticians, barbers) or those engaged in the "sporting life".

1. See Table I.
2. See Table II.
3. This phrase, which refers to the contiguous 48 states, is the outgrowth of the fact Alaska was the 49th state admitted to the union. As such, its people often searched for ways to distinguish themselves from the citizens of other states.
4. See Table III.
5. Referred to in the 1950 U. S. Census as Eastchester Village.
6. Created by State Statute in 1963.

CHAPTER III
THE WAR YEARS, BUILDING FOR DEFENSE

Attitudes held by a number of senior grade officers in the military and the social conditions existing in the United States in the decades of the thirties and the war years between 1941 - 1945 were reflected in how black troops were recruited, stationed, trained or deployed.[1] All these factors were manifested in the assignment of black troops to Alaska.

Ulysses Lee's book, The Employment of Negro Troops, published by the Office of Military History of the United States Army gives a complete treatment to how these factors impacted black troops in the service of their country in the years leading up to and during World War II.

The pretense of this chapter is not nearly as noble in its intent or substantive in its detail as that of Mr. Lee's work. The purpose is only to chronicle what were the general conditions nationally, and specific conditions under which black troops, assigned to Alaska, had to serve.

The two major projects black troops worked on

in the great Northwest were the Alcan Highway and the Canol Oil project. The Alcan project was designed to provide a direct overland link between the contiguous states and the Alaskan Territory. The Canol project was designed to provide an oil supply source close to Alaska. Both were considered crucial to the defense of Alaska.

Much of the historical records herein discussed were researched by military historian, Charles Hendricks of the Office of History, U. S. Army Corps of Engineers.

Attitudes harbored by a number of white officers in the thirties and war years, reflected a carry over from World War I. These attitudes were manifested in policy that impeded the integration of America's armed forces until the late forties. Also, how black troops were deployed at the time sustained the perception that blacks were not suited for combat duty or technical assignments.

As suggested, the attitudes exhibited by a number of white military commanders in senior level positions at the advent of World War II are traceable to perceptions formed by them as junior grade officers in World War I or the writings of military leaders of that era.

Typical of the times, as revealed in the memoirs of Maj. Gen. Robert Bullard which were published in 1925, in recalling his war years, he wrote, "Poor Negroes! They are hopelessly inferior." These attitudes held for blacks lead him to conclude, "Negroes were simply failures. If you need combat soldiers, and especially if you need them in a hurry, don't put your time upon Negroes."

To the credit of the nation's press, accounts are that it gave equitable coverage to the exploits of black troops during World War I. Newspaper coverage and expressions of gratitude by the government of France are in stark contrast to the attitudes expressed by a number of American military officers of the day. However, for the record it should be noted that not all white officers held blatantly racist attitudes and many worked for military reform.

The Boston Post under a banner headline, No Color Line There, commented, "In the service of democracy there is no such distinction. General Pershing's late report places on the roll of honor the names of two soldiers of one of our colored regiments, Private Johnson and Roberts... This is the true ideal of services. No matter what the color of skin, we all recognize it. The French government awarded the Croix de Guerre to three of the regiments of the 93rd Division during World War I."

The variance between news accounts with that of attitudes expressed by a number of white officers contributed to the confusion over what was the true performance record of black troops during World War I. This confusion was still in existence at the time planning was taking place for the United States entrance into World War II.

Manpower studies undertaken by the War Department in 1937 attempted to address the mistakes made in World War I. The plan proposed that from M-day (Mobilization) on, Negroes and whites should be mobilized in proportion to population. The approved nine point plan was not without controversy. The plan had the effect of placing a disproportionate number of blacks in the Infantry, Engineers, and Quartermasters Corps. From the time the plan went into effect and the outbreak of World War II, the net result was that every fourth man in the Corps of Engineers, and every sixth person in the Quartermasters Corps was black. As will be discussed later, this fact was in evidence in the number of black troops that were assigned to the Alcan Highway project.

Concurrent with the implementation of military manpower plans, the black press, most notably, the Pittsburgh Courier, in 1938 launched a campaign for expanding opportunities for blacks in the military services. This campaign, with the support of black organizations of the day, produced two significant events. In September, 1940 a White House conference was held with President Roosevelt. At the meeting a text containing seven specific requests was presented. As implausible as point three of the plan must have appeared at the time it was presented, and while it was never acted upon during World War II, it has been a reality in military life for a number of years. The request was that "Existing units of the Army and units to be established should be required to accept and select officers and enlisted personnel without regard to race." The time frame in which these requests were made is significant. The requests were made just a little under two months before the national presidential election. The requests were not adopted. However, just two weeks before the election Col. Benjamin J. Davis, senior black officer in the Army, was recommended for promotion to Brigadier General; and William Hastie, Dean of the Howard University Law School and former federal judge, was appointed Civilian Aide for Negro Affairs to Secretary of War, Henry Stimson.

A little over a year later, Mr. Hastie was in the process of arranging a meeting between black editors and Army Chief of Staff, General George Marshall, for Monday, December 8, 1941. The importance of this date was to be understood only after the attack on Pearl Harbor by the Japanese on Sunday, December 7, 1941. To his credit, General Marshall kept his appointment with the press. Departing from a prepared text he stated, "I am not personally satisfied with it either." The statement was made in reference to the lack of progress for blacks in the military. However, shortly after the

General departed the meeting to attend the assembly where President Roosevelt asked Congress for a Declaration of War against Japan, a Colonel Householder read from a prepared statement the following: "The Army did not create the problem. The Army is made up of individual citizens of the United States who have pronounced views with respect to the Negro just as they have individual ideas with respect to other matters in their daily walk of life. Military orders, fiat, or dicta, will not change their viewpoints. The Army then cannot be made the means of engendering conflict among the mass of people because of a stand with respect to Negroes which is not compatible with the position attained by the Negro in civilian life. This principle must necessarily govern the Army not only with this subject of contention but with respect to other dogma be it religious, political, or economic. The Army is not a sociological laboratory; to be effective it must be organized and trained according to the principles which will insure success. Experiments, to meet the wishes and demands of the champions of every race and creed for the solution of their problems are a danger to efficiency, discipline and morale and would result in ultimate defeat."

Ironically the statement set the tone for the conditions under which blacks were forced to serve during the intervening four years.

The attitudes and conditions that awaited black troops destined for the Northwest mirrored those existing in the contiguous states. Perhaps more so, if the attitudes were typified by those of the U. S. Army Commander in Alaska, General Simon Bolivar Buckner, the son of a Confederate general his negative attitudes about race were legendary. Fellow officers often were apologetic in their tone when talking or corresponding with General Buckner about issues of race.

After the decision was made to build the Alcan Highway, Brigadier General Sturdevant of the War Department's Office of the Chief of Engineers wrote to inform General Buckner of the decision. In a letter dated April 2, 1942 he stated in part, "The sixth Regiment will debark at Valdez, proceed by marching to the vicinity of Slana on the Gulkana-Nebesna road and construct a pioneer road through Nentesta Pass and down the Tok River to the Tanana River and thence eastward along the north bank of the Tanana until it meets the 18th Engineers.

This sixth regiment is the 97th Engineers (General Service - colored). I have heard that you object to having colored troops in Alaska and we have attempted to avoid sending them. However, we have been forced to use two colored regiments and it seems unwise for diplomatic reasons to use them both in Canada since the Canadians also prefer whites. I hope, therefore, that you will not protest this action since I believe it would only cause delay, with no different result, because the urgency of the project prevents reduction of the force and all remaining white regiments are assigned to task forces. We are now organizing two of the white regiments especially for this job. We cannot organize two others due to limitations of time, containment space, and output of training centers.

It is planned to have the two colored regiments return to warmer stations south of latitude 49 next fall. They will be hard at work in two reliefs on a 20 hour schedule in out-of-the-way places and I cannot see how they can cause any great trouble."

General Buckner responded, in part, by writing, "I appreciate your consideration of my views concerning negro troops in Alaska. The thing which I have opposed principally has been their establishment as point troops for the unloading of transports at our docks. The very high wages offered to unskilled labor here would attract a large number of them and cause them to remain and settle after the war, with the natural result that they could interbreed with the Indians and Eskimos and produce an astonishingly objectionable race of mongrels which would be a problem here from now on. We have enough racial problems here and elsewhere already. I have no objections whatever to your employing them on the roads if they are kept far enough away from the settlements and kept busy and then sent home as soon as possible. I hope, however, that none of them will be placed at the points of entry, since here is where our principal problem will arise."

One could conclude these two pieces of correspondence speak volumes about what type of attitudes black troops faced in Alaska or the conditions under which they had to serve. Amazingly race, as a problem, was being spoken to in such disparing ways by the Commanding General of the Alaska Defense Command less than two months before Japan would invade Alaska in the Aleutian Islands.

Mr. Zelmer Lawrence was one of the civilians who worked on Elmendorf and Ft. Richardson military bases, just outside of Anchorage, in 1942 and 1943. Ft. Richardson served as command headquarters for General Buckner. Mr. Lawrence substantiated the fact of General Buckner's negative attitudes about race. He recalled General Buckner as a "Cocky, pomp and ceremony officer who did not care for blacks." In support of his statement Mr. Lawrence recalled how the first black soldier stationed at Elmendorf was assigned to an isolated section of base housing in which he was the lone occupant.

The Japanese invaded the Attu and Kiska Islands on June 3, 1942, nearly a week after the arrival of black troops in Alaska over a thousand miles away in Valdez, Alaska. It took Allied Forces over 15 months to dislodge the Japanese forces.

In just over half the time it took 44,000 American and Canadian troops to dislodge 8,000 Japanese troops from two islands, the work of the Alcan Highway had been completed by 10,607 troops of which 3,695 were black.[2]

Four engineering battalions, which were expanded to regimental strength prior to being assigned or after arriving in regions in Alaska and Canada during World War II were black. The units were the 93rd, 95th, 97th and the 388th.

Given the bases at which the units received their training or were stationed prior to coming to Alaska, it is easy to surmise that the training the units received was not related to coping with the climatic conditions of the great Northwest.

In fact, the policy on the use of black troops overseas was that they should not be sent to northern climates. However, the urgency of the Alcan and Canol projects necessitated the use of black troops. The low morale of black troops, as accounts indicate, was similar to that of their white counterparts. The morale problems were traceable to insufficient clothing, monotonous food, poor shelter and long tours of duty. Temperatures during the winter of 1942, after the completion of the Alcan, but before the troops moved out, were recorded as low as 79° below zero.

Historical records indicate the overall performance of the units, in spite of morale problems, was meritorious.

The 93rd Engineers Battalion was activated on February 10, 1941 at Camp Livingston, La. It was expanded and redesignated 93rd Engineers Regiment (General Service) on March 28, 1942.

The 93rd sailed to Carcross Yukon Territories via Seattle in late April of 1942, arriving in May. The units first assignment was cutting in the road from Carcross, Yukon Territory to the Teslen River over fifty miles away. The unit received a Meritorious Unit Commendation, streamer embroidered for its service of the Alcan Highway project and received campaign participation credit for its service in the Aleutian Islands of Alaska. The unit also served in New Guinea during World War II.

The 95th was constituted as Regular Army in August of 1933 and was activated on May 15, 1941 at Ft. Belvoir, VA. The 94th arrived at Dawson Creek, British Columbia on May 27, 1942 and departed Canada on April 26, 1943.

The units first assignment was to begin road work between Fort St. John and Fort Nelson. Along with the 341st Engineers, they completed 36 miles of road before the end of June. The unit's service was also cited as meritorious.

The 97th Engineers Battalion was constituted in October of 1933 in the Regular Army as the 56th Engineer Battalion (Separate). The battalion was activated in June, 1941 at Camp Blanding, Florida. On March 11, 1942 it was reorganized and redesignated as the 97th Engineers Regiment (General Service).

The 97th arrived in Valdez, Alaska on May 7, 1942. By June the unit had started work on a section of road from Slana to the junction of the road traveling south from Fairbanks. After the completion of its initial assignment in Alaska, it was charged with completing the section of the Alcan Highway from Fairbanks south to White Horse, a distance of 500 miles. Military records indicate much of the road went through areas previously not visited by man. By September of 1943 the men had completed their assignment and set up a temporary camp at the White River to await the arrival of the units that were working on the Canadian section of the highway.

Operating heavy equipment on the Alcan Highway Project, Circa 1942

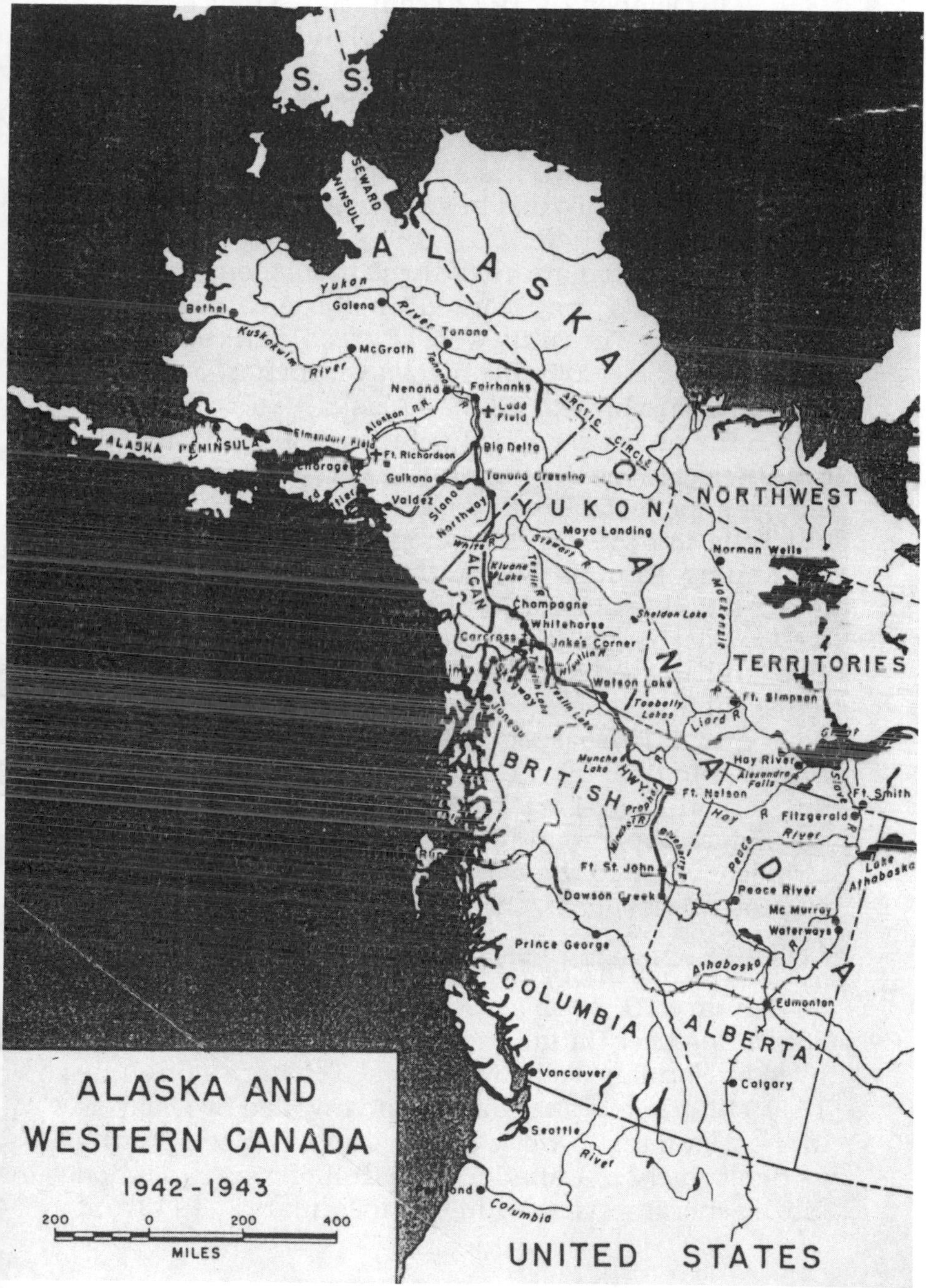

ALASKA AND WESTERN CANADA
1942 - 1943
200 0 200 400
MILES

On October 25, 1942 Technician 5 Refires Sims, Jr. of the 97th and Pvt. Alfred Jalufke of the 48th Engineers met with their bulldozers, thus completing the pioneer road from Dawson Creek in Canada to Big Delta in Alaska less than eight months. After completing work on the road, the 97th operated terminals for trucks utilizing the road before departing from Alaska in the Spring of 1943.

The citation awarded these units along with the white regiments that worked on the Alcan Highway project reads, "The units were charged with the task of constructing a 1,600 mile highway from Fort St. John, British Columbia, to Slana, Alaska, with all speed within the physical capacity of the troops. The general route selected for the highway lay across vast areas of almost impenetrable wilderness, vaguely mapped, and but little known. Commencing with the Spring and continuing through the summer floods, the troops overcame the difficulties imposed by mountainous terrain, deep muskeg, torrential streams, heavy forests, and an even lengthening supply line. By virtue of remarkable engineering ability, engineers improvisation, and unsurpassed devotion to duty, the units assigned to the highway construction completed their mission in one short working season, and thereby opened a supply road to Alaska that is of inestimable strategic value to the war effort of their country." The citation was issued by the War Department on April 15, 1943.

The 538th Engineer Battalion was first activated on January 10, 1942 at Camp Clairborne, La., as the 388th Engineer Battalion (Separate). The battalion arrived at Norman Wells, Northwest Territories on June 15, 1942, 12 days after Japan had invaded two islands in the Aleutians to work on the Canol project. During its deployment in Canada, the battalion was expanded into a general service regiment on January 1, 1943 and redesignated into the 388th Engineer General Service Regiment. The unit departed on August 30, 1943. The 388th later served in Normandy and Northern France and the Phillipine Islands.

Development of the Canol project was considered crucial to the military defense of Alaska. The project was designed to supply oil resources near Alaska. This need was defined in April of 1942 by President Roosevelt. Military strategists hoped that the project would be capable of producing several thousand barrels of oil a day by the fall of 1942. To accomplish the mission required the development of water, docks, rail, roads, pipeline and refinery systems.

The site of the oil fields was a distance of 500 miles from the site of the proposed oil refinery at White Horse along the route of the Alcan Highway in the Yukon Territories.

The military signed contracts with oil companies, construction contractors, and engineering firms to develop the project in May of 1942. Military personnel was to be used to improve the transportation system from Waterways to Norman Wells, the site of the oil fields.

When the 388th first arrived at Waterways in June, because of the climatic and geologic conditions, work on permanent facilities could not begin until the tundra thawed later in the summer. Thus, the troops were housed in tents. Their first assignments were to unload the great quantities of material and equipment that were being shipped into Waterways and begin work on living quarters.

In spite of the total commitment by all concerned, it became apparent in late June of 1942 that the project schedule could not be met. However, work continued on the project at a fever pitch. After completing its initial assignments, troops of the 388th were assigned to road building operations. By the fall of

1943 they had helped to bulldoze nearly 600 miles of road. The completion schedule continued to slip. After the 388th completed its work along with other units, in the late summer of 1943, the project became a totally civilian operation. After completion of the project and before its operations were suspended in April, 1945, the Canol project produced over a million barrels of oil.

Ironically, black troops served with distinction in remote regions on two projects of critical importance to our nation's war effort without knowing the extent to which the deck was stacked against them. They were patriotic pawns in a master plan for utilizing their service in isolated locations, so as to have their service be acceptable to a military commander possessed by racists attitudes.

Prologue:

With the passage of time has come progress. Black non-commissioned, and commissioned officers have served in many leadership positions at the bases that once were commanded by General Buckner, to include that of Base Commander.

1. Afro-Americans were referred to as Colored in military correspondence during World War I, and as Negro in correspondence generated during World War II.
2. The Alaska Highway, a report compiled for the CG ASF (May, 1945), II, OCMH. climatic conditions of the great Northwest.

CHAPTER IV
NIGHTLIFE

The establishment of the first black nightspot was made as an accommodation to heightening racial tension.

In the mid-1940's black citizens were coming to Alaska in increasing numbers, and the military was continuing its build up after having suffered the indignity of Japan occupying Alaskan territory during World War II.

The influx of people created a need for social outlets. Because of the disparity in the number of males to females, which for the non-Native population ranged from nearly two to three and a half to one[1], tension was generated between males vying for the attention and company of females. Ethnic differences was sometimes a contributing factor to the tension.

City fathers, wishing to stem race related tension, through the person of Harold Brown, founder of the Anchorage Daily News, approached Zelmer Lawrence and asked him to consider the proposition of receiving the support he needed to open a club that catered to blacks. The deal was cut and the Club Ebony was opened in 1948 at the corner of 5th/ Cordova Streets.

For several years Club Ebony was the only nightspot controlled by blacks. The club closed its doors in 1953. Ironically the basis for the need to open the club was lost in the "goodtimes". As pioneer Alaskans recall, the club provided an atmosphere for interracial socializing with none of the accompanying tension that existed elsewhere in town.

From the mid-fifties to the mid-sixties, as Alaska transitioned from a territory to a state, nightlife was at its zenith.

During a period of time when the permanent black population living in Anchorage totaled less than 4,000 people, blacks controlled over a dozen nightspots that were open 24 hours a day, and seven days a week.

Also, Tony Thomas assumed ownership of the Polar Hotel on 5th Avenue during this period of time. Later, she married Jack Ford in the early sixties and they constructed the Ford Building on 15th Avenue just east of Hyder Street, and opened the Brief Encounter night club in the facility.

Danny Gibson, who first came to Alaska in 1948, ran Ruby's Cafe restaurant on the first floor of the hotel. He opened the "Mermaid Room" on 5th Avenue in 1959. The club was still going strong in the late sixties after the clubs in Eastchester Flats had given way to urban renewal.

"Alaska was a lot of fun back then. Several of us business persons got together and decided to start a summer hardball baseball league. While two of the guys got on the plane to go "outside"[2] to recruit ball players, old man Lewis and I started to construct the baseball diamond." The field they worked on later became Mulcahy Park. Danny's team won several of the early league championships. The league has grown in

Jerry Phillips, tending bar at the Mermaid Room, Circa 1964

President Nixon being greeted by Danny Gibson during a stopover in Alaska during his trip to China in 1972

stature over the years. Since its inception in the summer of 1962, over 90 former and current major leaguers have played in Alaska to include Chris Chamblis of the Atlanta Braves and Dave Winfield of the New York Yankees.

Jerry Phillips, a former bartender at the club, remembers that the club kept two bartenders and five waitresses busy all the time. Jerry, a retired Teamster, now manages the Living Room membership club, for the Alaska Black Caucus located at the corner of 13th and Gambell in the building owned by the LeViege family.

Looking out at the Anchorage skyline from the club, he recalled, "You know a lot of today's stars used to come to Alaska when they were just starting out. Lou Rawls, and the Ike and Tina Turner Revue played the Mermaid Room."

Also located, within what was then the city limits, on 5th Avenue was the A & D Rhythm Club owned by a woman whose first name was Doria. She was murderd in the early sixties. The motive of the murder was robbery since it was a well known fact that she carried her cash receipts home with her for depositing in the bank the next day. However the robber only managed to reach the front porch of her house before dropping dead from gunshot wounds Doria was able to inflict before dying.

The Wyoming Bar was also located in the downtown area. The bar, which also had a rooming house attached, was owned by the Kilpatrick family. Pat Kilpatrick, the matriarch of the family, passed away some years ago. One of the sons, Lincoln, left the state and has enjoyed success as an actor. One of his roles was that of a detective on the popular television show of the mid eighties, Matt Houston. Another son, John, and his wife, Virginia, along with their children and grandchildren still make Alaska their home.

Lincoln Kilpatrick, noted movie and TV actor.

Clubs located just east of the city limits, which was Gambell Street, in Eastchester Flats, included Lucky's Hotspot, which was owned by Lucky Taylor, who legend has it got on the plane heading back to his native Louisiana with a suitcase full of money. His departure came after he realized the glory days of a wide open territory was giving way to the values of statehood.

Alberta "Bum" Penneywell, a pioneer Alaskan reflected on the times to be had in the Eastchester Flats during the fifties and early sixties. "I accompanied a cousin, who was returning to Alaska after recovering from an illness up here in 1950." Shortly after arriving, she met the family of people that she had known in her hometown of East St. Louis, Missouri. The family turned out to be the most famous furriers in Alaska, David Green Furriers. As friendships developed, a short visit turned into a thirty seven year residency.

"My husband, Jim, and I were married in 1952. Shortly thereafter, we assumed control of the C Shop Package Store. We lived next door to the store, and our place served as an unofficial party house."

Her comments clearly support the fact that Alaska was a territory. "Some people were still wearing guns on their hips. However, we did not have to lock the doors to our business or house." She cited two particular instances that dramatized the sense of community that existed at the time. "We returned from an overnight trip and found a note and money on our kitchen table." As it turned out, a group of soldiers had gone into the liquor store, taken some bottles off of the shelves, and stopped by the Penneywells' house to party. They cleaned up the place and left the money for the liquor they had consumed. Another time she recalled was when the first Governor of the State of Alaska, Bill Egan, stopped by to have a few drinks in the early sixties, got to telling stories, and rather than risk traveling, after downing a few, he spent the night on their living room sofa. Bum concluded the conversation she was sharing over her kitchen table, as her husband, Jim, was relaxing in his recliner chair with the family dachshound by stating , "The only change in Alaska that I feel any remorse about is that the people seem to have lost their sense of community, and as a result they are not as friendly as they once were."

Jeanette Johnson took over operation of the North Starlight Lounge after her first husband passed away in 1959. "We leased one side of the building to a fellow that operated a soul food place he called "Moms". When asked how the place got its name, she replied, "He used to have his mother cook the food. However, since he was unwilling to pay his mother anything for working in the cafe, he thought the least he could do was name the place after her."

Jeanette remarried. Along with her husband, Fred Johnson they relocated the club to its present location at 17th/Gambell in 1967 to accommodate urban renewal activities in the Eastchester Flats. The opening act was a group called the George Duke Trio. This gentlemen currently enjoys considerable fame in the field of jazz.

Over the years, her club, under a variety of formats, has hosted a number of entertainers to include Jimmie Smith, the jazz organist and the Staple Singers.

The area has turned into a prime commercial area with the state's largest bank opening one of its major branch offices adjacent to her property, and the Municipality constructed its 9000 seat Sports Arena directly across the street from the club in 1984.

Jeanette and Fred were divorced in 1977. He went on to devote time to a number of civic organizations to include a stint as Chairman of the Board of Directors of the Alaska Black Caucus.

Jeanette continued to acquire property in the vicinity of the club, which is now called the Crazyhorse. She probably controls more square footage of commercial land than any black in Alaska. The Crazyhorse, and another club she controls near the Air Force base, provides employment for over fifty people. At the time she was being interviewed, the good looking lady from Texas, was taking a lot of teasing from her friends over the fact she had just brought her oldest daughter a new Mercedes Benz as a college graduation gift. She was taking the ribbing in stride and laughing at herself about the present as contrasted to how naive she was when she first started out in the business back on 1957. "You know a women could not tend bar unless her name was on the license back then. I was just learning the business when a gentlemen came in one day to order a drink. Drinks were selling for 90 cents a shot then. He said, 'I want a shot of scotch and make it on the double.' I poured the drink I thought he was asking for and told him that would be $1.80. He looked at me like I was crazy and immediately proceeded back to the office where my husband was at the time to complain. He said I was attempting to charge him $1.80 for a shot that should cost 90 cents. I told my husband that he ordered a shot on the double so I was charging him for two drinks. After they were finally able to contain their laughter, my husband explained to me that a shot on the double meant that the gentlemen wanted fast service, not two drinks. Ever since that date, whether a person orders one drink or spends $3,000 a night setting up the bar, I instruct my people to give them service on the double."

Other clubs were located on a street that is now named Fireweed Lane. The street was the first major street south of the city limits.

The Club Oasis was located several miles outside the city limits on the Seward Highway. The club

Jeanette Johnson, with her son, Leroy, Circa 1962.

The Blue Room & O.K. Corral Nightclubs Owner, Pete Aiken. Fairbanks, Alaska

Jeanette Johnson, second from right, with her family, former husband, Fred, far left, their children (l to r) Fabrette, Jenada, & Leroy.

was owned by Josephine "Momma Joe" Evans-Smith. Lawanda Page, who later co-starred as Aunt Esther on one of the most popular television shows of the seventies, Sanford and Son, performed as an exotic dancer at the club.

Entertainers just starting their careers, and others who were nearing the end of theirs performed in Alaska during the late fifties to include Billie Holiday.

Noted entertainer, O. C. Smith of "Little Green Apples" fame, while serving in the military performed in a number of clubs in the Fairbanks area in the early sixties. He, along with his wife, Robbie, returned to Alaska in 1982 to perform at the Alaska Black Caucus Solidarity Banquet in the summer of 1982.

A popular nightspot in Fairbanks, Alaska during the time was the Club Timberline. The club was operated by Raymond Wright. He is recalled by persons living in Fairbanks as one "tough dude". Legend has it the police were afraid to go into his club. Whenever there was a disturbance, the police waited in the parking lot until things quieted down and Raymond came outside to let them know if things were okay. In the early sixties, he was found dead behind the bar in his club with his money bag in his hand. Obviously, the motive for the killing was not robbery.

As has been typical of every expansion of America's frontiers, territorial pioneers were tolerate of a lady's right to work, and people gambling. The attitudes toward these activities are recalled by people as one of benign neglect. Further, these activities were socially integrated.

There were a number of procurers of the day. Each controlled a stable of black and white ladies.

Frank, a person who still cuts a dashing figure, after an up and down career as a hustler, which has spanned five decades, recalls over a 4th of July Bar-B-Q gathering, "After finishing up my probation period,

O. C Smith's appearance at the Sheridan Hotel Grand Ballroom, Summer, 1982.

I'm going to leave Alaska." When asked what he was finishing up time for, he replied, "I was set up on a weapons and drug possession charge. You see I was out on probation for procuring, and I was running a little after hours spot in Fairbanks, when the police used one of my customers to plant a gun and one gram of cocaine in my place. When they staged one of their periodic raids, in addition to finding my usual liquor cache, they, as it turned out, also knew just where to go and look for the gun and "coke". After they took me in, they offered to cut me a deal if I helped set up some known dealers. I wasn't interested in any deal, since I was not involved in drugs and also did not plan on becoming an informer. Therefore, I did the time." After returning from the picnic table with another helping of ribs, he finished up his story. "Man, you couldn't believe the opportunity to hustle money that existed up here back in the late forties. You know the military guys could not bring their families up here with them back then. When I hit town in 1948, I went to the railroad yard and bought me a box car, and had it trucked to a little piece of land I had in the Eastchester Flats. I made it into a two bedroom unit and had my ladies start work. Within a month I had to add several rooms to the place just to keep up with the business. Also during this time, my buddy who was in the service used to let me borrow one of his uniforms so I could go on the base and get into the crap games. I used to be pretty good at "pad rollin". Between the crap games and my ladies, I made $40,000 within two months of hitting Alaska. I'm going to miss the lifelong friends I made, but the violence that has come to Alaska in the last decade, I ain't going to miss at all."

A famous Madam of the time also laughingly recalls how innocently the activities of gambling and "tricking" were looked upon at the time. "I served as a Madam of the house just outside of the city limits. You know, Della, the most famous lady of the day, and the other girls planned their calendars around the 1st and 15th of the month." As it turns out these were the dates that military personnel were paid, and also these were the dates when workers at remote construction sites hit town. Men with money, and the disparity between males and females over nineteen years of age, which at the time was nearly two to one, provided a ready clientele for the ladies.

"It was nothing for a girl to earn up to $3,000 a night on a pay weekend for the military", she recalls. "During the rest of the month the girls had their regular 'townie' clients. You know what? The girls used to classify the customers into the categories of big spenders, and cheapies. The Air Force personnel were categorized as big spenders, and the Army men were called cheapies. Locally, doctors and lawyers were big spenders, and bankers were cheapies. The girls would argue all the time about whose turn it was to party with a known cheapie."

Hardly able to contain her laughter, she states, "One day when I was outside planting flowers to make the house look more like a home, this prominent dentist comes out of the house with nothing on but his boxer shorts, and walks over to the fence around the yard, with his knobby knees knocking. About this time a cab pulls up. The dentist gave the cab driver some instructions and turned to walk back to the house. As he passed me I asked him what that was all about." He said, "I sent the cabbie down to my office to get some more money because I'm not ready for the party to stop."

Statehood changed a lot of things. It outlawed B-Girls[3] and the bars were required to close at 2:00 a.m. By the time the economic damage of these requirements were assessed, a lot of places had gone out of business. The requirement was amended to 5:00 a.m.

However, by this time a colorful era had passed. Girls who once were grossing in the thousands a month, and people who were playing in neighborhood poker games where the pots were up to $20,000 a hand have become a thing of the past.

Pioneers also recall the fact that a Reverend Grant of First CME, a disabled Korean Conflict veteran, often talked with the men and women of the evening in an attempt to have them consider Christianity as an alternative lifestyle. While he had mixed success in converting people, he was very successful in gaining the support of these people to help his mission. A number of the men contributed to the fund to purchase a church at 529 F Street, and some of the ladies worked in the kitchen of the restaurant he set up in the basement of the church.

Looking out the window of her well furnished apartment, the still very attractive former Madam whose looks belie her age, states, "I still keep in touch with the people who befriended me when I arrived in Alaska. However, the lifestyle that I once engaged in is but a distant memory."

1. U. S. Census, 1950.
2. Is a term used to describe when persons travel from Alaska to destinations in the contiguous states.
3. Girls who worked in clubs were allowed to split the profits from drinks served with the bar owner.

CHAPTER V
PUBLIC SERVANTS

Since statehood, a number of blacks have been appointed to public service capacities at the State and Municipal levels. In every instance, these men and women have also found time to volunteer assistance to worthwhile community projects. Their service to humanity runs the gamut from serving on boards of youth and senior citizen organizations, which are not race specific, to advocating for the civil and economic rights of minorities.

Frank Austin, came to Alaska in the late fifties. He cites his story as being similar to that of many of the blacks who came to Alaska during territorial days. "You got so busy taking advantage of the opportunities and making a living that you took the problems in stride and moved on. While racial problems did exist, Alaska's boom and bust economic cycles were often the great equalizer."

He spent his first 24 years in Alaska with the Federal Aviation Administration (FAA). Before arriving in Anchorage in late 1961 he spent two years in Nome and 19 months in King Salmon. He started his FAA career in Alaska as an Air Traffic Controller in Nome and moved on to such positions as Equal Employment Opportunity Manager and Airport Planner. In 1982 he moved from the federal service to local government service with the Municipality of Anchorage. He currently serves as Director of Employee Relations for the Municipality of Anchorage.

Frank's professional career has not prevented him from participating and contributing many hours of community service. In his more than 23 years of community service he has held such diverse positions as President of the Alaska Congress of Parents and Teachers (State PTA) and Representative to the National PTA Board of Managers, Member of the Alaska Real Estate Commission, Member of the Alaska Public Offices Commission, Chairman of the Borough Economic Development Committee and Chairman of the Municipal Personnel Review Board. Frank also founded the Anchorage Chapter of Blacks in Government (BIG). He was selected as Caucus Member of the Year by the Alaska Black Caucus in 1980.

His wife, Ruby, recently retired after 30 years in education. The last 23 years of her career were spent as Head Librarian at Chugiak High School. Prior to that she had taught in such other Alaskan locations as Naknek, and on Prince of Whales Island.

Frank says the high points of his life in Alaska were the opportunity to vote for statehood in Nome and his survival of the 1964 Earthquake. He was in the Air Traffic Control Tower at Lake Hood during the earthquake. The Austins have raised three sons.

For 17 of the 20 years Jewel Jones has lived in Alaska, she has worked for the Anchorage local government. Jewel was asked to join the city government by former Mayor George Sullivan who, at that time, was concerned that blacks, minorities and women were not properly represented in the city work force. Beginning with a grant from the Federal Department of Labor called New Careers, she was responsible for ensuring the hiring of over one hundred minorities and women, many of whom are currently in city government in both management and supervisory positions. New Careers was responsible for recruiting the first black police officers, fire fighters, telephone operators, and engineers in the city work force.

In 1975, Jones became Director of the Social Services Department for the City which included day care, employment, housing programs, the Affirmative Action, and Contract Compliance functions for the City.

In the fall of 1983, the Departments of Social Services and Health and Environmental Protection were merged with Jones being appointed Director. These expanded duties included all the former responsibilities plus oversight of community health clinics, family planning, abuse prevention, air and water quality programs, Animal Control, and block grant monitoring with non-profit agencies.

During an interview, she was posed the question, what is your pet peeve? She answered by stating, "I'm somewhat remorseful over the fact our community, as well as Anchorage at large, has not demonstrated the commitment necessary to elect a black to the Municipal Assembly."

James Chase tenure with the University of Alaska Anchorage has presented a number of challenges, as well as obstacles yet to be overcome. Shortly after assuming his position in 1979, he initiated administrative policy reform that brought sorely needed objectivity to the recruitment process for administrator and faculty members. However, systematic discrimination as personified in the "good old boy" network for internal promotions, has effectively denied advancement to minorities and females.

PUBLIC SERVANTS
TABLE V

NAME	POSITION	YEARS OF SERVICE
Frank Austin	Various Positions	1958 - 1982
	Federal Aviation Administration	
	U. S. Government	
	Director, Human Resources	1982 - present
	Municipality of Anchorage	
Jewel Jones	Director, Social Services	1970 - present
	Director, Health & Human Services	1983 - present
	Municipality of Anchorage	
Jan Ridgeway	Assistant Municipal Librarian	1972 - 1987
	Construction Manager, Z. J. Loussac Library	
	Municipality of Anchorage	
Carol Smith	Affirmative Action Officer	1974 - present
	Municipality of Anchorage	
James Chase	Director, Human Relations	1975 - 1977
	Municipality of Anchorage	
	Director, EEO	
	University of Alaska, Anchorage	1979 - present
Carolyn Jones	Attorney	1975 - present
	Attorney General's Office	
	State of Alaska	
Ted Chenier	Deputy Purchasing Director	1976 - 1987
	Purchasing Director	1987 - present
	Municipality of Anchorage	
Dan Robinson	Superintendent	1975 - 1980
	Deputy Director	1980 - 1982
	Chugach State Forest	
	State of Alaska	
Charlie Mae Moore	Teacher Certification	1979 - present
	Department of Education	
	State of Alaska	
Charles LeViege	Director, EEO	1978 - 1981
	Municipality of Anchorage	

PUBLIC SERVANTS
TABLE V (con't)

NAME	POSITION	YEARS OF SERVICE
John Seabrook	Director, EEO Anchorage School District	1979 - present
Walt Lawson	Director, Administrative Service Department of Public Safety State of Alaska	1983 - present
Ed Rhodes	Deputy Chief of Police Municipality of Anchorage	1982 - present
Willie Sykes	Director, Office of Enterprise State of Alaska	1983 - 1984
Remond Henderson	Director, Administrative Service Community & Regional Affairs State of Alaska	1983 - present
Mel Henry	Director, Mental Health and Developmental Disabilities State of Alaska	1983 - present
Lewis Sears	Assistant Commissioner Dept. of Health & Social Services Municipality of Anchorage	1983 - 1985
Donald Barlow	Deputy Fire Marshall Anchorage Fire Dept. Municipality of Anchorage	1985 - present
Cal Williams	Investigator Equal Rights Commission Municipality of Anchorage	1986 - present
Ed Smith	Statewide Director Affirmative Action University of Alaska	1986 - present
Charles Moses	Director South Central Region Department of Corrections State of Alaska	1987 - present

Carolyn Jones, a Stanford Law School graduate, has served in the State of Alaska's Attorney General's Office for a dozen years.

Her stint as counsel for the State Commission on Human Rights for nine years resulted in a number of landmark discrimination cases being resolved in favor of the plaintiffs. She was a finalist for consideration for appointment as a state judge in 1980. However, she was passed over by then Governor Hammond for a male. As of the summer of 1987, no black has ever been appointed to a judgeship.

Dan Robinson, after retiring from military duty, worked for seven years in a public service position. Since his second retirement, he has been an unpaid lobbyist for the interest of the black community with the state legislature. He is an active member of New Hope Baptist Church.

Charles LeViege came to Alaska with his two brothers and sister in the early sixties.

After enjoying a successful athletic career at Alaska Methodist University, since renamed Alaska Pacific University, he went into banking. He served as a construction loan officer, and later as a branch manager. He resigned his management position with the National Bank of Alaska, and assumed management of his family's growing paint business. The business enjoyed considerable commercial success.

In the late seventies he heeded the call to public service issued by Mayor George Sullivan[1] The Mayor, in responding to the concerns of minority and women groups, supported the concept of establishing an Office of Equal Opportunity. The Office reported directly to the Mayor. He was charged with the responsibility of promoting Affirmative Action, and developing a Minority Business Enterprise Program. He drafted both the enabling ordinance (79-161), which was adopted by the Municipal Assembly on September 11, 1979, and the

Jewel Jones Addressing the Alaska Black Caucus. To her left is former U.S. Senator Mike Gravel. Winter, 1980

program which was administratively adopted by Mayor Sullivan shortly thereafter.

He left Municipal service in early 1982 after sensing a lessening of commitment to the program by incoming Mayor Tony Knowles[2]. History should note his intuition was correct. The office was downgraded, and it no longer reports to the Mayor's office. As Mayor Knowles nears the end of his second term, the office is viewed as being virtually ineffectual by the minority business community.

Charles now devotes time to his commercial interests. He and his wife, Dulany, have two sons and two daughters.

After serving for twelve years in the Municipality of Anchorage's Purchasing Department, Ted Chenier was appointed to the position of Purchasing Director in the summer of 1987. During its last fiscal year, the department coordinated the letting of contracts for goods and services totaling $275,000,000.

John Seabrook, in his capacity as Director of the Office of Equal Opportunity with the Anchorage School District, has made measurable contributions to the most progressive public agency in the state for providing equitable employment opportunity for blacks, females, and other minorities.

Dr. Lewis Sears took a leave of absence from his position with the Anchorage School District to serve in the Sheffield Administration. After completing a tour of duty with state government, he returned to an administrative position with the School District. He and his wife, Betty, have two children.

Don Barlow, a 15 year employee of the Anchorage Fire Department, was promoted to the position of Deputy Fire Marshall in 1985. He is active in church and community affairs. He is currently serving as President of the Anchorage Branch, NAACP.

Cal Williams' exploits in the late sixties and early

seventies represented a changing of guard in the type of leadership in the community when he assumed the presidency of Anchorage Branch, NAACP. Subsequent to his activist activities, he has served in leadership capacities with the State Democratic Party.

John Alexander has a career history in the labor field. He was the first black to ascend to a cabinet level position in state government when he was appointed Commissioner of Labor by the late Governor, Bill Egan. He was one of the founders of the Alaska Black Caucus and served as its first vice-president. He was appointed as Director of the Office of Equal Opportunity in the Office of the Federal Inspector in Washington, D. C. when indications were that the proposed Alaska Natural Gas Pipeline would be constructed in the late seventies. When the project was postponed, he returned to Alaska and was appointed as Director of Labor Relations with the Municipality of Anchorage.

Karen Cory arrived in Alaska in September of 1973 from Knoxville, Tennessee. A graduate of the University of Tennessee, she was selected as a Special Assistant to Governor Jay S. Hammond. She served in this capacity from March, 1979 through 1983, with 1980 and 1981 spent as Chair-person of the Alaska Pipeline Commission. In 1983, Karen was appointed as the Regional Director of the State Commission on Human Rights. Ms. Cory's additional activities during these years included lay member of the Alaska Bar Association, officer of the Alaska Republican Women's Club, and coordinator for the White House Conference on Families.

Ms. Cory left government service in December 1984 to establish a private consulting firm.

Dr. R. London Smith was one of the first cabinet level appointments Governor Bill Sheffield made when he took office in late 1982. Dr. Smith is a retired military officer who left a tenured teaching position in

PUBLIC SERVANTS
Governor's Office / Cabinet
Table VI

NAME	POSITION	YEARS OF SERVICE	GOVERNOR
John Alexander	Commissioner of Labor	1974	Bill Egan
Karen Cory	Special Assistant to the Governor	1979 - 1983	Jay Hammond
R. London Smith	Commissioner of Health / Social Services	1983 - 1984	Bill Sheffield
Henry Lancaster	Special Assistant to the Governor	1983 - 1984	Bill Sheffield
Jim Kelly	Special Assistant to the Governor	1984 - 1986	Bill Sheffield
Eleanor Andrews	Commissioner of Administration	1985 - 1986	Bill Sheffield
Ray Price	Special Assistant to the Governor	1986 - present	Steve Cowper

the Political Science Department at the University of Alaska, Fairbanks to serve in the Sheffield Administration. He remained in the position for less than two years. The reported reason for his resigning was the frustration he experienced in attempting to make changes in the bureaucracy. He and his wife spend their time traveling between Fairbanks and their vacation home in Hawaii.

Henry Lancaster, who helped to research portions of this book, during his tenure as Special Assistant to Governor Bill Sheffield, was able to secure grant funding for several community based programs. He also made a breakthrough when he got administrators in the Division of Tourism to place advertisements with a black national publication. He left his position to seek public office in the fall of 1984.

Jim Kelly, who after retiring from the military, operated a number of successful enterprises to include a residential care home, prior to being appointed to fill Lancaster's position. Jim is now bouncing back from a stroke he suffered during a plane trip in late 1986. He and his wife, Parnell, are active in a number of public affairs.

Eleanor Andrews, Commissioner
Department of Administration
Sheffield Administration

On June 26, 1985, when she was appointed by Governor Bill Sheffield to head up the 1,200 person Department of Administration with its annual budget of $160,000,000, Eleanor Andrews became the first black female to serve in a cabinet level position in State Government.

She was raised by her mother and stepfather in Los Angeles. She did not get to know her father, Jimmie Williams, until she journeyed to Alaska in 1964 after meeting him for the first time in 1961. She arrived in Alaska only several days before the 1964 earthquake. Her father earned his living by traveling throughout the territory in pursuit of a gambling career in the forties. He later built a successful painting business in Fairbanks.

Blessed with a great sense of humor, she recalled her first job in Alaska, "I went to work in the meat department of a Safeway Store in Fairbanks. I used to unload 50 pound packages of bologna off a truck and then work in the freezer for hours. When I would get off work dogs and cats would follow me home because I smelled like raw meat."

Her marriage to John Andrews produced a son, Christopher, and a daughter Marti. Her daughter's birth, was somewhat unique, in that she was born in a cab on the way to the hospital. Marti has been traveling ever since. She is now living in Germany. Her son lives in Paris.

When posed the question, What has been the secret of her success?, she replied, "I have never allowed myself to accept the full burden of race. I think a lot of black women have a sense that, I must present myself for our race. This is a lot of pressure. So it is like you have these certificates for the black population. Some black women are driven, as we all are, by a sense of inadequacy. You have to be superwoman to be anybody. A lot of people have that hang-up, but can you imagine an entire race? That is a lot of baggage. You are either wonderful or nothing."

Ray Price, who served as the director of Steve Cowper's Anchorage Campaign Office, was appointed to a Special Assistant's position in the Governor's Office after the election. Subsequent to the election, in addition to working to find a solution to the dreadful problems existing in the Department of Transportation and Public Facilities, he has had to deal with a lot of community pressure. The black community has become disenchanted with the Cowper Administration for its failure to fund any community based programs, or make a representative number of appointments of blacks to his Administration. Governor Cowper's actions have been mystifying to a number of prominent community leaders who signed on early in 1986 to help his campaign knowing they were taking a substantial risk in attempting to unseat an incumbent Governor, who by comparison in hindsight, has proven to be much more honorable in keeping campaign promises.

Because the community realizes that Ray Price is working hard trying to turn things around, he has maintained his position of respect in the community.

1. Served as Mayor of the City of Anchorage from 1967 - 1975. Upon unification of the Borough and City into the Municipality of Anchorage, he was elected Mayor and served two terms, 1975-1981.
2. Mayor of the Municipality of Anchorage, 1981-1987.

CHAPTER VI
POLITICOS

Since Alaska became a state in 1959, less than fifteen blacks have served in elective capacities.

Currently 560 elective public offices require that a conflict of interest statement be filed with the State of Alaska Public Offices Commission. At the end of 1987 only five blacks were holding public offices. This figure represents approximately one percent of the total number of persons serving in elective office.

The Alaskan Legislature is a bicameral body. Forty persons serve in the House of Representatives and twenty in the Senate. In the history of the state only five blacks have served in the body; all in the House of Representatives.

The Legislature meets annually, usually for not more than 120 days. Because of this fact, it is viewed as a citizen's legislature. People serving in this body have historically brought to the job a wide variety of educational, professional, and civic involvement experiences. Blacks who have served, or are serving in the legislature have backgrounds quite similar to their majority and Native counterparts. All sponsored legislation that addressed the important issues of their era.

Blanche McSmith, the first black to serve in the legislature, brought to the job a wealth of community involvement. She helped to found the Anchorage Branch, NAACP in 1951. She served seven years as its second President. She was appointed to fill an unexpired term in the Legislature in 1960.

During her short stay in the legislature, she was the prime sponsor of nine pieces of legislation.

Willard Bowman, who passed away from cancer in late 1975, arrived in Alaska in the late forties. After serving for five years as the Executive Director of the Alaska Human Rights Commission, he was elected to the State House in 1970. During the year he served in the legislature he sponsored or co-sponsored 120 pieces of legislation. Mr. Bowman is survived by his wife, Maria, and their children, Williard Jr., and Gregory Warren.

Josh Wright, a graduate of Howard University's School of Dentistry served in two public capacities. After retiring from public life, he gained financial independence by maintaining a successful dental practice for over two decades, and by developing a number of prosperous real estate ventures.

He remains active in civic affairs and enjoys his role of elder political statesman in the black community. In early 1987 he was a nominee for the Chamber of Commerce's prestigious "Alaskan of the Year" award.

He and his wife, "Mitch", a registered nurse, raised two sons, Josh and Rodney, and a daughter, Jackie.

During his time in the legislature he sponsored a number of bills in support of education. He was a member of the House's important Finance Committee.

Selwyn G. Carrol, remains the only black from Fairbanks to have served in the state legislature. He

STATE OFFICE HOLDERS
TABLE VII

NAME	OFFICE HELD	YEARS SERVED
Blanche McSmith (D)[1]	State Representative	1960
Willard Bowman (D)[2]	State Representative	1970 - 1975
Josh Wright (D)	State Representative	1971 - 1972
Selwyn Carrol (R)	State Representative	1973 - 1974
Walt Furnace (R)	State Representative	1982 - present

(D) Democrat, (R) Republican

1. Appointed to seat. Did not win re election.
2. Died while in office.

came to Alaska in the late fifties. Prior to serving in the legislature he was employed as a social worker and juvenile counselor in the State's Department of Health and Social Services. Also, he taught in the Fairbanks School System at the secondary level.

During his time in the legislature he sponsored or co-sponsored legislation dealing with employment security and economic development.

Walt Furnace, a native of Ennis, Texas, came to Alaska as a member of the U. S. Air Force. After fulfilling his military obligation, he took an entry level position with the National Bank of Alaska. After rising through the ranks to the level of branch manager, he left the bank to start a small business consulting firm. Prior to being elected to the State's House of Representatives, he served on the Anchorage School Board to include a term as its President. Running as a Republican, he was elected by a substantial margin for an election district that is upwards of 95 percent white. During his first term, he was a member of the majority coalition and chaired the House's powerful Labor and Commerce Committee.

President Ronald Reagan is greeted by Rep. Walt and Mrs. Pat Furance during the President's stopover in Alaska in 1983 on his way to the Far East.

In 1983 he was recognized as one of the nations most promising legislators.

During his first five years in office he has sponsored legislation dealing with taxation, regulations dealing with the professions, and housing loans.

In the summer of 1987 he hosted the Western Regional Annual Conference of the National Black Caucus of State Legislators. Among those participating were Dave Richardson, National President from the state of Pennsylvania, Elihu Harris, Theresa Hughes and Gwen Moore of California, and Gloria Tanner of Colorado. The conference was addressed by Alice Huffman of California on education issues, and a number of oil industry personnel spoke to the need for support of exploration of the Alaska National Wildlife Refuge (ANWR) for possible energy reserves. The conference was concluded by a keynote address by Willie Brown, Speaker of California Assembly, at a banquet held in conjunction with the Alaska Black Caucus.

He and his wife Pat have three daughters, Samantha, Carmellia, and Tara.

Vince Casey, prior to and after his tenure on the Anchorage School Board, has served in a number of appointed public capacities to include those of Executive Director of the Municipality of Anchorage's Equal Rights Commission, and a Director of the Office of Equal Opportunity. He is recognized as being a strong advocate for neighborhood self determination.

Before serving on the Anchorage School Board, Ed Rhodes had built a reputation such that he was considered one of the most respected state troopers in Alaska's history. He resigned from the Board because his duty station was transferred outside of the Municipality, he was appointed to the position of Deputy Chief of Police in the Administration of Mayor Tony Knowles in early 1982.

Bettye Davis arrived in Alaska 15 years ago as

LOCAL OFFICE HOLDERS
TABLE VIII

NAME	OFFICE HELD	YEARS SERVED
Pete Aiken	Fairbanks Borough Assembly	1961 - 1967
Joe Marshall	Fairbanks City Councilman	1971 - 1982
Jim Hayes	Fairbanks School Board Fairbanks City Council	1973 - 1975 1987 - present
Walter Johnson	Fairbanks Borough Assembly	1987 - present
Rosalee Walker	Juneau City Councilwoman	1986 - present
Josh Wright	Anchorage School Board	1969 - 1972
Vince Casey [1]	Anchorage School Board	1972 - 1977
Ed Rhodes [2]	Anchorage School Board	1977 - 1978
Walt Furnace [3]	Anchorage School Board	1978 - 1982
Bettye Davis [4]	Anchorage School Board	1982 -present

1. Resigned to accept an appointment as Director, Municipality of Anchorage's Equal Rights Commission. Served as Board President, 1976 - 1977.

2. Resigned because of a change in duty assignment as a state trooper.

3. Resigned to run for State Legislature. Served as Board President, 1979 - 1980.

4. First appointed to seat. Served as Board President, 1985 - 1986. First black woman elected to public office in Alaska's history.

the wife of a career military husband. From the time she arrived in the state she has been active in the civic, social, and political affairs of Anchorage. From the late seventies and through the decade of the eighties, she has served in a number of leadership capacities. As the decade crossed its mid-point, she had assumed the unquestioned position of pre-eminence in the black community. In the early eighties she was encouraged by leaders in the community to seek appointment to a vacant position on the Anchorage School Board. After serving in the appointed post, she recorded a historic first, in 1983, for black females by becoming the first of her gender and race to win a public election. In 1985 she was re-elected without opposition and became Board president in the same year.

Bettye retired from her position as a professional social worker in the State's Department of Health and Social Services in 1986. She viewed her retirement, while still in her forties, as an opportunity to perform more public service for the citizens of Anchorage. She is a graduate of Grambling State University, and often publicly praises her husband, Troy, son, Tony, and daughter, Sonya, for their support and encouragement.

She was nicknamed the "steel rose" by one of her closest friends in admiration for her toughness under pressure, yet being possessed with a sensitive and caring nature.

During a summer of 1987 gathering of civic, business, and political leaders, in her role as Chairperson of the Alaska Black Caucus, she gave a critical assessment of black America.

"Once again it gives me great pleasure to extend greetings to the attendees of our 11th Annual Solidarity and Awards Banquet. It is quite fitting that we assemble ourselves to reaffirm our freedom and belief in economic parity for all people.

Black America has made tremendous progress but we must not become complacent because the struggle is still on. It should not come as a surprise that even though slavery has been officially over for more than 122 years, we still find ourselves struggling against slavery under new guises: racial discrimination in this country, apartheid and colonialism abroad.

Today, even as we assemble here, we find ourselves a race in a struggle for survival. One out of every three blacks in this country is officially listed below the poverty line. One out of three blacks lives in substandard housing. One out of five black adults is unemployed. One out of every two black youths can not find work. Despite the progress we have made in the area of voter participation, less than two percent of the more than 600,000 elected officials are black. In the House of Representatives there are a total of 22 black Congress-persons, including the non-voting delegate from the District of Columbia, out of 435. In the United States, since the defeat of Senator Edward Brooke, there are no blacks out of 100 Senators. Of the top Fortune 500 Corporations, less than 130 have blacks on their Boards of Directors. Black enrollment in medical schools is less than five percent and in dental schools less than three percent of the total. The life expectancy for black Americans is six years less than that for whites. The black median income is 58 percent of that of white families.

I cite these figures to highlight the fact that although we have made tremendous progress in the area of race relations, we still have a long way to go and contrary to the glib assertions made by many, much remains to be done if blacks are to share in the economic wealth and prosperity of this nation.

On behalf of the Alaska Black Caucus, I challenge each one of you to join us in our struggle to make the world a better place for all races. Keep the wheels of progress turning. Enjoy yourselves, stay committed to bringing about positive change and remain intellectually honest to your beliefs and values. My sincere thanks and best wishes to all."

Fairbanks, Alaska's second largest city, in addition to sending Selwyn Carrol to the State House have had four other blacks serve in public capacities. Jim Hayes served on the Fairbanks School Board in 1973 - 1974, and was elected to the Fairbanks City Council in 1987.

Jim is a product of the Fairbanks School System. He stands well over six-three, and weighs over two hundred thirty pounds. He looks more like a person who would be finishing out a professional football career as a defensive end, than someone who is a member of the Fairbanks City Council. He is a soft spoken person. He measures his words carefully. His words and deeds indicate he is well aware of the fact that black progress will have to be sustained through economic and political empowerment. His wife, Chris Parham Hayes, while not aspiring to any elective political office, is very active in community organizing activities and is blessed with the courage of her convictions. During a town meeting held in August of 1987 she stated, "We as blacks have become too complacent, and now seem unwilling to challenge injustice. This problem is particularly acute in public sector employment."

Walter Johnson, a stockbroker won a seat on the Borough Assembly in 1987.

Joe Marshall served on the city council from 1971 to 1982. His removal from office by the Alaska Public Offices Commission in 1986 outraged his supporters, and black leaders state-wide. The basis for his removal was the late filing of a campaign financial disclosure statement of a campaign that required only six hundred dollars to finance. However, members of the council re-appointed him to the seat he had to vacate. Joe passed away in the mid eighties. His eleven years in public office remains the greatest length of time served by a black.

Stella recalled with fondness Joe's public service. "We came to Alaska to work in construction. Joe's leadership qualities lead to his being appointed president of the Plasterers and Cement Masons Union in 1964. From there he was encouraged to run for elective office. For all of my 34 years in Alaska I have had some type of political or civic involvement. The need for blacks to organize is probably greater today than it ever has been." It should be noted that she has also found time to publish poetry. The Marshall's son Whitney is in college.

Rosalie Walker was the second woman elected to public office in the state when she won a seat on the Juneau City Council in 1986, after a career in state government and as a teacher.

Pete Aiken, who is still active in the business affairs of Fairbanks, served on the Borough council in Fairbanks from 1961 - 1967. He first came to Alaska in 1941 on assignment to a counter-intelligence unit. He returned in 1950 and has remained in Alaska ever since. He still takes a lot of teasing from his liberal friends who affectionately call him "Mr. Republican". Labels aside, his political involvement has benefited the community. His wife, Cynthia, serves on the Board of Directors of the Alaska State Housing Authority, and is the Director of a substance abuse program.

Bettye Davis Leading a march of students, along with teacher, Robert Boyd(l), and Rev. Rodney Pearson from Government Hill elementary School in recognition of the first national holiday in honor of Dr. Martin Luther King, Jr. in January, 1986

CHAPTER VII
RELIGION AS A CORNERSTONE

It is hard to reconcile the role religion has assumed in the lives of many black Americans, to include those in Alaska, with the acts that are currently being perpetuated in the name of religion both national and internationally.

Observing the acts and events associated with religion in the eighties, there is little comfort to be derived, if the salvation of humankind is contingent on responsible behavior being exhibited, moral and spiritual leadership being provided by the perpetuators of these acts and events.

As an example, the so called Moral Majority, which has its roots in the Southern Baptist Convention, has made a number of highly publicized political blunders, to include, pushing for prayer in public schools and backing hand chosen political candidates. After a short period of national exposure, the organization could not take the heat of "high stakes" politics and as a result its efforts to mix the affairs of state and church have frizzled. It's leader, Jerry Falwell, has moved on to what appears to be greener pastures called the PTL Club. As everyone in the Western World must know by now the couple that was leading this organization, Jimmy and Tammy Bakker, were removed from their leadership posts for moral indiscretion and emotional duress. Their ouster would seem to support the conclusion that confessing ones sins and asking for forgiveness is no longer an acceptable religious teaching or practice.

During this period of time another preacher, Oral Roberts, who depends very heavily on electronic evangelism to sustain his operations, claimed that God was going to take his life if he didn't raise a certain amount of money within a specified period of time. To dramatize his situation, he locked himself in a tower. Miraculously, the money was raised that allegedly saved his life. However, as faith would have it, he did not stop at fund-raising, he has recently professed that he can raise the dead.

However, these comedic religious events, pale in comparison in the acts of aggression that are being committed in the name of religion elsewhere in the world.

In Northern Ireland, religious fanatics are committing barbarous acts against their fellow country-persons. In the Middle East, religious teaching is the brainwashing tool used to poison the minds of generation after generation.

It should be noted that strife resulting from people and nations with religious differences is not a latter 20th century phenomenon.

History is replete with examples of the senseless extermination of human life because of religious intolerance.

Unfortunately, religious teachings afflict many of us with parochial paranoia. This affliction is caused by people accepting without question the definition by leaders of what constitutes good versus evil.

Even in an advanced and enlightened society, most of us go along to get along because of the fear of being ostracized. A tribal need to cultivate a sense of belonging is the prime reason leaders are able to manipulate people, especially those who profess a higher calling and have a working knowledge of religious antiquities. This fact in many instances precludes any serious dialogue which leads to broader understanding and increased levels of human tolerance.

Admittedly, the author's Methodist upbringing, causes inner conflict in attempting to reconcile the fact that much of societal unrest or oppression is based on religious differences and failing to understand why leaders of organized religion have failed to stem these transgressions.

Anyone growing up in a church setting has to accept the reality that between 11 a.m. and 1 p.m. on Sundays are the two most segregated hours of the week in the United States.

The black religious experience in the United States differs in fundamental ways to many of the current events. However, it also reinforces the fact that religious worship is also a wholly segregated practice in this country.

The essence of the black religious experience in America was captured in a statement by Congressman Walter Fauntroy, who is also a Baptist minister, during his visit to Alaska in 1984. Before a capacity audience, he made light of the fact that it appears "white men gave black folks religion and they took the rest of the country for themselves."

After the laughter at the truth finally subsided, people began to reflect on the subliminal message of his statement. The reflection leads one to conclude that on the one hand, the black church has been our most

BLACK CHURCHES
TABLE IX

CHURCH NAME	DENOMINATIONAL	LOCATION	PASTOR
	ANCHORAGE		
Anchor	Church of God	437 E. 14th	Abe Jeter
Antioch	Church of God in Christ	1211 Karluk	W. A. Webb
First CME	Methodist	36th / MacInnes	Harold Harrington
Greater Friendly Temple	Church of God	6310 DeBarr	C. D. Williams
Greater Friendship	Baptist	13th / Ingra	J. L. Smith
Leake Temple	Methodist	430 N. Hoyt	Ted Moore
New Hope	Baptist	333 Price	Carl Johnson
Shiloh	Baptist	855 E. 20th	Alonzo Patterson
	FAIRBANKS		
Lilly of the Valley	Church of God in Christ	29th / Barnette	Leroy Parham
Corinthian	Baptist	23rd / Lathrop	Samuel Banks
St. John	Baptist	17th / Turner	Charles Barlow
First AME	Methodist	23rd / Mercer	L. Cleaver
First C. G. C.	Church of God	308 Ladd	Ivory Thorthon
True Victory	Baptist	(North Pole)	V. Reed
St. James AME	Methodist	Southside Ctr.	Charles Brown

stable institution. On the other, a number of our religious leaders have been too slow in meeting the challenge of change. Given that these leaders control the minds and emotions of many of our people, their dated teachings have in a number of instances had a handicapping effect on our march for progress.

If we are to speed up our rate of progress as a people, our churches must move beyond simple and irrelevant teachings and mobilize their following in support of political, social and economic activism as a part of the modern religious experience.

Fortunately, the black religious experience in Alaska is in marked contrast to many national and international events.

The 1950's saw an increase in the number of families arriving in Alaska. This increase created a need for a place in which families could worship.

Saint John Baptist Church, Fairbanks

Lily of the Valley Church, Fairbanks

First AME Church, Anchorage, Alaska

Shiloh Baptist Church, Anchorage

Today there are eight predominantly black churches in Anchorage and seven in Fairbanks[1]. From the beginning these churches have attended to the spiritual and social needs of its members. The spiritual leaders have assumed a variety of other leadership roles in the secular community.

The primary forum for training and promoting leadership has been the Anchorage Interdenominational Alliance of Ministers, Deacons, and Stewards. The group was formed in the summer of 1973 to serve as a theological institute, and an advocate for social action. Over the years it has trained a number of young people in the Christian faith.

Also, leaders of this group have spoken out on important issues to the community. Of particular note has been the concern for the use of deadly force by the Anchorage Police Department. Depending on the leadership and with varying degrees of success, the group has attempted to educate its members about political issues.

The growth of black churches can be traced back to the early fifties.

In 1952, in the basement of the First Baptist Church, whose congregation was predominantly white, through the assistance of its pastor, Rev. Griffen, Rev. Kennedy conducted the first services for black worshippers. A short time later, arrangements were made for services to be held in the Pioneer Hall at 3rd/Eagle. Out of this effort came the formation of Greater Friendship Baptist Church.

Shiloh Baptist Church was formed by persons emerging from Greater Friendship Baptist Church.

Sunday, May 25, 1952 marked its beginning. Thirty persons assembled in the Carpenters' Hall to organize the church. Rev. John N. Deforre, at that time Pastor of the Calvary Baptist Church, presided at the meeting. Rev. J. L. Holiday was elected the first pastor.

Mrs. Anne B. Smith, Secretary, Governor Chamblis, Willie Hurt, Willie Leslie and J. K. Davis were elected the first deacons. Several days later another meeting was held in which Thomas A. Lewis, W. O. McGee and Henry Burton were elected to the Board of Trustees. At this same meeting Velma Smith, Ola B. Leslie, Verna Mae Nealy and Amanda Gaines were elected to the Deaconess Board.

During Rev. Holiday's pastorate, worship was moved to the basement of the site at 229 West 8th Street. In 1954 Rev. B. H. Gibbs served as interim pastor until Rev. N. L. Presley arrived from Oakland, California. Rev. Presley served until 1956.

Rev. D. S. Chandler of Monroe, Louisiana was pastor from August 1956 until October 1957. Under his administration the walls of the main auditorium were completed.

Rev. Murdock, pulpit chairman, carried on services until the election of Rev. E. M. Howard in March 1958. Approximately six months later the inside work of the main auditorium was completed, and dedication services were held the third Sunday in October 1958. Rev. Howard served until the first Sunday in August 1965.

Rev. Giles Trammel served as interim pastor from December 1965 until January 1966, when Shedrick Griggs, who had been ordained by Rev. Trammel was elected to serve as temporary pastor, and being elected pastor in July 1966 serving until his untimely death in February 1970.

During this interval Rev. G. H. Simien and Rev. J. H. Turner and others carried on the services until November 1970 when Rev. A. B. Patterson of the Corinthian Baptist Church, Fairbanks, Alaska was elected to the pastorate, being duly installed July 1971.

Shiloh's new church home was dedicated on August 8, 1976. An educational wing was completed in 1982.

The person who has lead the growth of Shiloh for the past seventeen years, Dr. Alonzo Patterson, Jr., is universally respected, if not always appreciated by Alaskans.

He was born and received his public education in New Orleans, Louisiana. He was ordained a minister in August, 1960 in San Antonio, Texas. Over the years he has continued his education at both undergraduate and graduate levels.

After a tour of duty in service to his country as a member of the U. S. Army, he founded Corinthian Baptist Church in Fairbanks, Alaska in 1970. Since assuming the spiritual leadership of Shiloh, its congregation has grown to number in excess of a thousand members.

Because he is equally adept at being a spiritual leader and a community activist, he is viewed by many as a man for all seasons.

With great fluidity he's able to provide leadership in all aspects of religion, advocate for social justice, and relate in no uncertain terms the aspirations of the black community to the host of elected or public office seekers who beat a daily path to his door.

He serves in a host of public capacities to include the position of President of Greatland Baptist State Convention of Alaska; Instructor for the Congress of Christian Education; National Baptist Convention, USA, Inc.; President, Alaska Black Leadership Conference; Chairman, Martin Luther King Holiday Committee; President, Interdenominational Ministerial Alliance; and Chairman, Parole Board State of Alaska.

He is married to Shirley Patterson and is the father of five children.

Anyone who talks with him immediately gains an appreciation for the fact that his beliefs are bedded on an unshakable foundation of spiritual values.

During an interview the question was asked

what does he believe to be the greatest need of blacks in Alaska? He pondered the question for a short period of time and responded by saying, "Unity, that can only be fostered by a sense of roots. Our cultural base is primarily rooted elsewhere in the country. We need some landmarks in Alaska that will promote and sustain our cultural development as a people."

When asked if it would offend him to be referred to as a Christian activist, a smile came over his face that gave every indication that his spiritual values and his human experiences have long since allowed him to move past dealing with how others may refer to him as he pursues his mission in life. "You have to accept the fact that when you attempt to move mountains you are going to disturb someone's property. In a political context this translates into a loss of innocence and popularity. Further, given that Martin Luther King, Jr. and Adam Clayton Powell have influenced how I view my commitment to serve humanity, it should not be hard to understand why I would not be offended by anyone calling me a Christian activist."

"Politics in Alaska often does not fit comfortably into standard patterns. In a number of instances, I have been disappointed by liberal sounding Democrats, who you could not turn-a-round without bumping into them at any gathering with more than five persons, expressing their commitment to progress. Yet, ironically it's been two Republicans that have kept their word to me. Namely, Rep. Walt Furnace, and former State Senator, Bill Summer."

The interview was concluded with the question about how he would like to be remembered. Without hesitation, he replied, "I would like to be remembered as a Christian who was willing to carry the ministry of Christ beyond the walls of the church to impact the social order of things."

A mission to establish the First Christian Meth-

Reverend A. B. Patterson, Jr.

odist Episcopal Church was sent to Anchorage, Alaska in 1959. The Mission was appointed by Bishop F. L. Lewis. Members consisted of Bishop Claude Allen, Gary, Indiana and the Rev. N. S. Curry, Editor of the Christian Index, Jackson, Tennessee.

Rev. James A. Covington, former pastor of Miles Memorial C.M.E. Church, Tacoma, Washington was appointed as the church's first pastor. The church was organized on July 5, 1959 in the Pioneer Hall at 3rd and Eagle. Present and joining were Walter Bremond, Lillian Wells, George Anderson, and Ruby Dorough.

On October 11, 1959 First C.M.E. moved out of the Pioneer Hall into a newly established building located at East 12th Avenue and Denali. The Good Friday earthquake of 1964 forced the church to relocate. On August 1964 the property located at 529 F Street became First CME's new church home. The church was purchased by the Municipality in late 1984 and demolished so the site could be utilized as a town square.

The first service in the new facility at 36th and Mac Innes was held on December 24, 1986. The building was dedicated on Sunday, May 24, 1987. Presiding Bishop E. Lynn Brown of the Ninth Episcopal District conducted the dedication services. Accompanying Bishop Brown to Alaska was a contingent of out of state guests to include Reverend Borens of Oakland California and Dr. I. Carlton Faulk, Secretary Lay Department. Persons representing the church on its building committee were Rev. Jesse Wilson, Leona Holloway, Howard Gee, and Chairman, Ron Givens.

Rev. Harold Harrington was appointed church pastor in August.

The New Hope Missionary Baptist Church had its humble beginning in the Carpenters Hall on Easter Sunday, April 1960. Officers were borrowed from the Anchorage area church community, under the leadership of Rev. Earnest Smith, and organized by Elmendorf A.F.B. Captain J. A. Harkness, Chaplain.

Mom Bessie Higgins, borrowed from Shiloh Missionary Baptist Church, became the acting Sunday School Superintendent and continued in the position for 13 years.

Bob Davis served as usher; Ann Davis played the piano; and J. D. Mullins acted in a dual role of deacon and chairman of trustees.

On May 8, 1960, twenty one persons joined the Church. Among those faithful few came the following officers: Deacon Dan Hawkins, Deaconess Vallie Mae Hawkins, Deacon Willie Hurt, Deacon Willie Johnson, Deaconess Juanita Johnson, and Deacon Robert Brooks. Original members who continue to worship with the New Hope Family are Bessie Higgins, Vallie Mae Hawkins, and Robert Brooks.

In 1963, New Hope moved into the basement of its present Church building. In that same year, its Pastor, Earnest Smith, passed.

In 1962, Deacon Paul Sharp and Rev. Gaskins were licensed into the ministry.

Rev. Boyd Rogers served as pastor from 1963 to 1966. In 1966, William B. Lyons came from Fairbanks to lead the church.

On July 1, 1976, a ground-breaking ceremony for educational space and sanctuary enlargement was held. A re-dedication program for this addition was held on January 23, 1977.

From 1978-80, Pastor Lyons served as President of the Alaska State Baptist Convention. He was the first black minister to ever be accorded such an honor.

On January 23, 1984, Pastor Lyons passed away. In October, 1984, the Municipality of Anchorage established the William B. Lyons Park, adjacent to the Church grounds in his memory.

In 1984, Rev. John Smith became the interim pastor. On January 20, 1985, Carl Johnson was appointed pastor. He began his official duties on Sunday, March 3, 1985.

Prior to coming to Alaska, Rev. Carl Johnson, held positions at the Ninth Street Baptist Church in Lawrence, Kansas, from May 1970 March 1976. His second position was at the Park Avenue Baptist Church in Kansas City, Missouri, from March 1976 1984. He holds a B.A. in Business Administration from the University of Missouri; and M.R.E. from Central Baptist Theological Seminary, and a Doctor of Ministry from the St. Paul School of Theology in Kansas City, Missouri. Carl has held District and State office in the National Baptist Convention. His father, the Rev. A. L. Johnson, served as President of the Convention for Kansas-Missouri. Carl served in the U. S. Army for three years, and has teaching experience with the Western Baptist Bible College, and the St. Paul School of Theology, both located in Kansas City, Missouri. He and his wife, Helen Marie, have two daugthers, Arla and Dathne..

When posed the question, beyond providing spiritual leadership in his Church, how would he characterize his ministry? "I would say its one where I recognize the need to shift from an autocratic style of leadership to one of lay empowerment. Especially in the areas that deal with administrative and secular outreach functions a modern day church must be involved in order to remain spiritually relevant, and viable in an economic sense."

"The building program we are about to embark on will represent a classic case study in this regard."

His doctoral dissertation[2] clearly reinforces his views about promoting positive change in the management of the church while maintaining control over the spiritual aspects of the church. However, even in this regard as one of his other papers would support, he is unafraid to advocate for changes.

"For several years now, I have been in the process of expressing a conviction relative to full participation on the part of women in Christian ministry."[3]

Rev. Leroy Parham, a 72 year old minister, who looks years younger, is typical of persons that were called to the ministry in Fairbanks. He first came to Alaska in the early fifties to work in construction. While driving a truck to support his family, he tended to the special needs of a growing community. His growth as a minister has paralleled that of the community. His church is in the final stages of completing a major addition.

Also, it is inevitable that some preachers of the gospel will continue to confine their responsibilities to the narrow view of religious dogma. Whereas, others will view their responsibilities as including the need to provide spiritual leadership as well as secular enlightenment for their followers. History supports the latter type as having made fundamental contributions to blacks' progress.

As it has for the past thirty five years, religion will continue to play a significant role in the lives of black Alaskans.

1. See Table IX.
2. "The Chronicle of a Pastor at Risk", Rev. Carl Johnson, February 23, 1986.
4. "Call Waiting", Research papers submitted in partial fulfillment of doctoral requirements, Rev. Carl Johnson, February 23, 1985.

CHAPTER VIII
SOCIO/ECONOMIC ISSUES

The socio/economic issues faced by blacks in Alaska, in a number of instances, are similar to the issues that challenge our counterparts in the "Lower 48".

The prime public social/economic issue that on the surface has been successfully challenged is that of equal access. The prime socio/economic challenges that remain are those of eliminating obstacles to equal employment opportunity in state government and developing a stable and viable business community.

Framers of the Alaskan Constitution, in the mid-fifties, were aware of the growing number of racially motivated incidences between whites and Native civilians, and black military personnel.

The Constitution of the State of Alaska was adopted by the Constitutional Convention on February 5, 1956, and ratified by the people of Alaska on April 24, 1956. It became effective upon Alaska being admitted to the Union on January 3, 1959.

Article V, Declaration of Rights, Section 3 (Civil

Rights) states, "No person is to be denied the enjoyment of any civil or political right because of race, color, creed, or national origin[1].

Just a little over four years after Alaska became a state it became evident that an organized approach would be necessary to enforce Article V of the Constitution.

In 1963 legislation was passed creating a State Commission for Human Rights (Commission) in the Office of the Governor. The enabling legislation's intent was that the Commission be more than a simple complaint taking bureau. The mandate was to have the agency seek out and eradicate discrimination in employment, in credit and financing practices, in places of public accommodations and in the sale, lease or rental of real property. Willard Bowman, whose career as a representative has been previously reported, served as the Commission's first executive director.

Throughout its history the Commission's effectiveness, relative to the speed in which it resolves complaints, has been a "sore spot" with community groups and activists. In a number of instances, groups and individuals found it necessary to resort to direct public action and the resulting publicity to seek timely resolution of instances of discrimination. However, to the Commission's credit, it has demonstrated a willingness to tackle large institutional problems.

There exists two classic cases in the foregoing regard. Blacks picketed a food store chain, Carrs Quality Centers, in 1962. Also, in 1978, the Commission charged that the State of Alaska was not promoting equal employment opportunities for minorities.

Today, Carrs Quality Centers is the state's largest non oil related business. Back in the early sixties, when the business was just beginning to grow, one of its outlets was located adjacent to the Fairview neighborhood. Spoke-persons for blacks who were beginning to build homes and become a viable consumer entity in this community accused Carrs of discrimination in its hiring practices. The store which is still located at the corner of 13th/Gambell did not employ any blacks. Informal meetings with the company's founder "Pop" Carr did not lead to any resolution of the issue.

To dramatize the situation, a picket of the store was organized by Clarance Coleman, Branch President of the NAACP, and Willard Bowman, in 1962. The black paper of the period, Sun Reporter, provided coverage of the boycott. Included among the people who walked the picket line, a quarter of a century ago, were Flossie Coleman, Susie Ford, Ella Mae Lockhart, Worthy Mack and Emma Stokes. The Lark's Club which was located at the corner of 13th/Hyder, served free meals to all the people who walked the line. Shortly thereafter, the issue of providing employment opportunities was resolved. Today under the leadership of "Pop" Carr's son, Larry, the business has become one of the most progressive in the state. Blacks are employed as store managers, and in various other administrative positions.

In early 1978 the Commission was charged with being ineffective by the recently established Alaska Black Caucus. This group along with a number of community activists presented the Commission with information indicating that the state itself was guilty of discriminatory practices.

Following several meetings between the Commission's staff and community leaders, the Commission forwarded a six page letter to Governor Jay Hammond[2] stating in part, "virtually no progress has been made in hiring minorities and women during the past five years, and the state is wide open to enforcement and fund cut-offs by the federal government." The letter also characterized the state's equal employment office as having failed in a miserable fashion.

In 1978 of the 457 state employees earning in excess of $40,000 only one was black; less than one quarter of one percent.

In early January of 1983, the state instituted an expanded certification hiring plan. The plan required that managers use an expanded applicant pool when filling vacancies in state job slots where minority and females were underrepresented. Any pool from which applicants were to be drawn had to include at least five minorities and five females. The plan was refinement of the one developed during the Hammond Administration, but implemented under the Sheffield Administration by Barry Best[3], Director of the state's Office of Equal Opportunity.

However, as to be expected in any organization, private or public, that has fourteen departments, and at the time nearly 15,000 employees, selective enforcement by insensitive managers rendered the plan virtually ineffective.

Figures released in the summer of 1986 documented that blacks are still grossly underrepresented in state government. Only 14 out of 2,000 state employees earning in excess of $50,000 were black; less than three quarters of one percent.

The prime offender in state government remains the Department of Transportation and Public Facilities (DOT/PF). Of the 131 employees in DOT/PF, in 1978 that earned in excess of $40,000, not one was a minority or female.

When the problems of the lack of employment and contracting opportunities in state government were scheduled for a hearing before the House Finance Committee in 1978, the chairman of the committee was Steve Cowper. During the hearing he voiced concern for the problems.

Mr. Cowper became Governor of Alaska in December, 1986. Ironically, as of December 1987, he has appointed only one black to a position in his administration and the problems are as plentiful as ever at DOT/PF.

Of the two hundred plus employees in DOT/PF who are currently earning in excess of $50,000, not one black is among this number.

DOT/PF has become a symbol of institutional racism to the black community. Suits and settlement agreements have not resulted in any improvement in this agency's hiring and contracting practices.

The fight for equitable participation in public contracting is crucial to socio/economic progress because Federal, State, and local governments pump hundreds of millions of dollars into the Alaskan economy annually. These revenue sources provide numerous contracting and service opportunities for private sector firms in a state whose population totals just over a half million people.

DOT/PF, because of the revelation of the depth of its problems, was mandated under the terms of the settlement agreement it entered into with the Commission on February 27, 1980[4] to compile employment and contracting data.

Part II, Provision 4, of the agreement mandated that DOT/PF "incorporate into its wholly State funded construction contracts in excess of $100,000 a system of reporting requirements similar to those appearing in federally funded contracts which would assist the Department in monitoring the equal employment practices and affirmative action commitments of its contractors and subcontractors. The Department agrees to furnish to the Commission a copy of the above reporting requirements."

A review of the reports on file with the Commission revealed almost non-existent opportunities in meaningful employment capacities for minorities and females, and that blacks' participation on contracts between the fiscal periods July, 1981 and July, 1987 never reached one percent of total contract awards.

Further, participation summary figures reported for minority and females were over represented and inaccurate.

These findings were supported by a Legislative Audit, completed in 1986, entitled, A Report on the Department of Transportation and Public Civil Rights Office's Affirmative Action Employment and Contracting.[5] Quoting from the report, "A recent internal report investigated and compared the actual amounts received by subcontractors with the subcontracts reported to DOT/PF by prime contractors.

The report found that there were some major discrepancies in the amounts reported for certain contractors. As a result, the actual goals achieved for some projects were significantly less than the goals committed to by the prime contractor."

Also, this agency compiled no records pursuant to the legislative intent of the Federal Public Works Act of 1977, and the Surface Transportation Act of 1982[6] which mandated ten percent be set aside for minority businesses on projects utilizing these funds.

Amazingly, this "shoddy" recordkeeping at DOT/PF has been allowed to exist for over half a decade under the same administrator without a change being made. This inaction alone speaks volumes about the depth of the problems at DOT/PF and within state government.

The discovery of the problem at DOT/PF, and the publicity surrounding its revelation, served as the catalyst needed to have black organizations, with different agendas, to develop a strategy to advance their mutual self-interests. The Alaska Black Leadership Conference (ABLC)[7] came into being as a response to the need for these groups to network statewide.

While the problems with DOT/PF were being exposed, Marva Williams, as Director of the Alaska Plan, along with Vertis Williams, her assistant, were waging a battle to gain membership in the craft unions. Their efforts met with a measure of success under difficult conditions. Howerver, bickering between union, Native and black members serving on the Plan's board for control lead to the devise of the program shortly after Marva and Vertis left the program to pursue other careers.

Given the Federal Government presence in Alaska, it is hard to understand its lack of enforcement of the laws relating to promoting minority and female business enterprises. Especially in light of the fact the Federal Government annually appropriates hundreds of millions of dollars that are utilized by state government. While the federal government has exercised little oversight over its annual appropriations, it has exercised tremendous influence over three landmark socio/economic issues in Alaska. Also, other issues are currently being subjected to the exercise of federal control.

Construction of the private eight billion dollar Trans Alaska Pipeline System (TAPS)[8] required both state and federal approval. The federal government was able to leverage its influence because of the fact the oil line crossed federal lands under the management control of the Department of Interior (DOI). Also, the commodity (oil) to be transported was subject to regulatory control by the Interstate Commerce Commission (ICC). The complicated process that needed to be completed prior to gaining federal approval is well beyond the scope of this book. As the problems at DOT/PF focused on the need for blacks to network statewide, our experiences with the oil pipeline demonstrated the need for us to network nationally.

When the issue was being considered by the

The Trans Alaska Oil Pipeline

Congress in the early 1970's, two black Congresspersons, Parren Mitchell of Maryland, and Yvonne Braithwaite of California,[9] were instrumental in having language added to the project enabling legislation that required the utilization of minority and female enterprises on the project.

However, history indicates that DOI was largely ineffective in enforcing these requirements. Only two fairly significant contracts out of the thousands that were issued went to black firms. Alaska Associates, a group of businesses located in Fairbanks, Alaska received a multi-million dollar contract to fabricate concrete anchors needed to hold the oil pipeline in place in locations where it traversed rivers and streams.

The Association was incorporated on June 17, 1974 by Maurice Bailey, Earnest Caston, Henry Gradney, U. C. Graze, Ernest Griffin, Jesse Griffith, Ellis Murray, Willie Ratcliff, Robert Taylor, and Joe Torres.

The other major contract was issued to a firm out of Kansas City, Kansas to provide catering service at one of the camp sites.

In addition to the lack of construction related opportunities, there were a number of reported instances of racial harassment of black workers at isolated work sites. The major offender was a union (Local #798) representing pipe welders based out of Oklahoma. This union has a monopoly of pipe welding services throughout the country.

Subsequent to the completion of the oil line in 1978, attention has shifted to a second major socio/economic issue, the proposed gasline.

The act that granted the authority to move forward with the development of the gas line was passed by Congress on October 22, 1976. The Reorganization Plan, Nov. 1, 1979, issued by the executive branch of government called for the establishment of the Office of the Federal Inspector. This office was

Congressman Parren J. Mitchell,
of Maryland's 7th District.

charged with promulgating rules to govern the construction of the line. Rules relating to the utilization of minorities were proposed in early 1979.

Congressman Mitchell fought for and the Alaska Black Caucus[10] provided testimony for the need to have the gas line project subject to all applicable federal laws governing the utilization of minority and female businesses. This coordinated effort was the first documented instance of a black state organization networking with a national leader to focus on the needs and plight of minority businesses in Alaska.

The gas, which is a by product of oil extraction, is being injected back into the ground until economics make it feasible to construct the gas line.

Also, in early 1980, a group of seven black men[11] journeyed to the nation's capital to speak to state elected officials serving at the national level, and other national leaders about conditions in Alaska. The group was received at the White House by Louis Martin, Special Assistant to President Carter. From there, several members of the group journeyed on to Richmond, Virginia to participate in a historic conference on a Black Agenda for the Eighties. This trip resulted in an Alaskan organization developing the ability to communicate directly with national black leaders of the day. During the intervening seven years a number of these persons have come to Alaska to participate in various programs, meetings, forums and hearings.[12]

The negative experiences of minority and female businesses during the construction of the pipeline, and charges made by a number of these firms that the local office of the U. S. Small Business Administration was employing a system of reward and punishment in certifying firms for eligibility in its various programs, led Congressman Mitchell to schedule a Congressional Hearing in Alaska in July, 1980.[13]

During the two days of hearings nearly fifty

Alaska Black Caucus members meet with Louis Martin, Special Asst. to the President. Pictured from left are Martin, B. Walker, Dr. C. Rolark(publisher of the Washington Informer), L. Overstreet, G. Taylor, F. Austin, H. Ahmad, F. Johnson, and S. Taylor.

minority and female business persons and representatives of federal agencies testified at the hearings.

The central theme underlying the hearings was to assess the effectiveness in which Public Law 95-507, which was enacted on October 24, 1978, and related federal minority business programs were being implemented. This law required the insertion of minority subcontracting plans in most federal prime contracts exceeding $500,000 or $1,000,000 for construction.

While the hearings were sorely needed in Alaska, and for those minority business persons who testified a gratifying experience, conditions, as discussion later in this chapter will document, have worsened in the intervening seven years.

The efforts of the Alaska Black Leadership Conference (ALBC), and publicity of the trip to Washington, D. C. by the group of seven men, resulted in Governor Hammond appointing one of the group to serve on a twenty-three person blue ribbon committee of prominent Alaskans to lobby Congress on the third major socio/economic issue that faced Alaska. At issue was how federal lands, in what amounts, and in what locations would be conveyed to the state and Alaskan Native Corporations?

The piece of legislation that was passed in this regard was Public Law 96-487, commonly referred to as the D-2 Lands Act.

Blacks were of the anticipation that by supporting the legislation, and lobbying members of the Congressional Black Caucus, as well as members of Congress of the majority culture that represented districts and states that have significant black populations, they would be rewarded with an improved business climate for blacks in Alaska. This anticipation was never realized. State officials have not demonstrated the creative leadership necessary to broaden the economic base in Alaska by lessening the state's dependency on tax revenue generated from the oil industry nor aggressively enforced the provisions of the law that deal with the utilization of minority and female businesses. Blacks continue to suffer a disparate impact, because of a lack of public sector jobs, as well as contracting opportunities, particularly in state government.

Also, in spite of the fact the state awards grants totaling millions of dollars annually, within the past decade, only four grants have been administered by blacks. Only two have dealt with minority business development, the Minority Business Enterprise Assistance Center in Fairbanks, headed up by George Taylor, and the Minority Resources and Services Center in Anchorage, chaired by Herb Turner.

Additionally, during his stay in Alaska Herb Turner has served in leadership capacities with Masonic and other groups. He and his wife, "Ness", have five children.

Also, there is no record of any meaningful business venture ever being undertaken between a Native Corporation and one black business firm. This experience is currently influencing how blacks view two issues that are before Congress in the summer of 1987.

The Native Claims Settlement Act, which was originally passed in 1971, and amended by P.L. Law 96-487, is back before Congress which is determining whether one of the acts more controversial provisions should be changed. In 1991, if no changes are made, individual stockholders in the Native Corporations would be able to sell their stock to non-Native individuals, or other entities.

While the general consensus is that the black community will not do anything in an overt manner to damage the position of the Native Corporations before Congress, leaders in the community are inclined to sit this one out or let the Natives fight their own battle.

However, the second major issue pending before

Congress, blacks anticipate on being very active. At issue is whether the Federal government should allow private enterprise to explore for oil on federal refuge land. The land in question is the Arctic National Wildlife Refuge (ANWR).

H. B. 1082 introduced in the 100th Congress on February 11, 1987 by Congressman Don Young, if passed into law would, "Authorize the Secretary of the Interior to lease in an expeditious and environmentally sound manner lands in the Coastal Plain of the Arctic National Wildlife Refuge for oil and gas exploration, development, and production." The bill has tremendous potential consequences for Alaska. However, since the bill is opposed by environmental groups, its fate is uncertain at best.

Support for the bill, which is co-sponsored by Congressman Mickey Leland, 18th District of Texas, in the black community is being coordinated by State Representative, Walt Furnace, Henry Lancaster and Charles McGee. During the summer of 1987 a series of meetings were held to assess the conditions under which the bill could be supported so as to further the economic interest of the state and enhance opportunity for blacks.

During October, 1987 Representative Furnace led a lobbying team to Washington, D. C. which included community leader and businessman, Bill Sykes, and the author of this book to develop an overall lobbying strategy with Alaska's Congressional Delegation members, Senators Ted Stevens, Frank Murkowski, and Congressman Don Young, as the bill works its way through the committee process. While in the nation's Capitol, thanks to the efforts of Chuck Bremer, a lobbyist for the International Electronics Workers Union, the team was also able to meet with Bill Gray, 7th District of Pennsylvania, Mike Espy, 2nd District of Mississippi, and Mervyn Dymally, 31st District of

California.

In early 1988 efforts by blacks in Alaska will be critical to the process of broadening the base of support for H. B. 1082. Already Congressman Dymally has indicated that he will introduce an amendment to the bill when it reaches the floor what would require 10 percent set aside for minority businesses. He also indicated to the lobbying team that based on additional input to his office by blacks from Alaska, principally through the person of Andonia Harrison of the NAACP's regional office, he will cast his vote in support of their position on the issue.

Business opportunities remain virtually nil. There exists two classic examples in this regard. The first example is the Linda Arms apartments, which was located in the heart of the Fairview Neighborhood which is one of the two most significant black communities in Anchorage. In the late fifties this complex served as the first place of residence for a number of blacks arriving in Alaska. The old complex was scheduled for demolition with a new complex rising in its place. The project, which was started in the late summer of 1980, was a multimillion dollar venture coordinated by the state, influenced by the Municipality and funded by the U. S. Department of Housing and Urban Development. In spite of numerous protests from the black community, the project was allowed to proceed with a blatant disregard for enforcement of applicable federal law.

This community project provided the most graphic example of why the black community needed to organize around socio/economic issues, rather than along political lines.

In the summer of 1984 the federal, state, and municipal governments again were intent upon cutting the black community out of a piece of the action on a project directly across the street from the site of the

Linda Arms apartment. Community leaders discovered that the S & S Apartments project was "wired" for a recently established nonprofit organization headed by a group ministers.

When the black community became aware of the governmental entities' intentions, it mobilized to stop the project. The community was able to leverage its position by making the project an issue in the mayoral campaign. The black community was able to shift support from the liberal incumbent mayor, Tony Knowles to his conservative opponent, Tom Fink. This issue had a significant impact.

While the election remained in doubt for several weeks, the incumbent mayor won re-election by less than 200 votes. However, because of the publicity the proposed project received during the campaign, it could not proceed in the manner originally orchestrated.

Today the site remains vacant. The re-elected mayor claimed victory by designating the site as a park, and the community claimed victory by stopping history from repeating itself.

The root causes of problems faced by blacks were put in succinct perspective by noted print and broadcast journalist, Tony Brown, during a visit to Alaska in 1982.

"If blacks are on the bottom of the political and economic ladders, there has to be a reason; for every cause there is an effect and for every effect there is a cause. The reason wc are oppressed is that we do not know where we have been. Therefore, we do not know where we are going. If we knew our true history, we would not accept the myth that black history began with slavery in this country. We should know that slavery is but a brief footnote in a people's history that began in the cradle of civilization. It's a myth that if we love ourselves, we hate whites." He went on to explain

Tony Brown, Host and executive producer of Tony Brown's Journal, made an appearance in Alaska in 1982.

how racism is a brand of ignorance that had been desegregated in America. This ignorance causes blacks to abet their own economic and political oppression. He concluded by stating, "If blacks knew their history, they could love themselves as much as they love other people. If we know our history, we would know it does not matter what name people call us. It is the name we answer to that matters."

The lack of black business participation in Alaska was addressed in dramatic fashion by Earl Graves, Publisher of Black Enterprise Magazine, during a speech he gave before a gathering convened by the Alaska Black Caucus of civic, business and political leaders in Anchorage during the summer of 1983.

In part he stated, "This annual banquet is becoming an important event on the calendar of black America because the examination and exchange of ideas that occurs during this annual period of 'Solidarity' sets the goals and aspirations for all of Alaska's minority citizens.

I have had the good fortune in my life to have participated in two of the most crucial chapters of American History. As an aide to the late Sen. Robert Kennedy and a friend of the late Rev. Martin Luther King Jr., I was able to lend my will and determination to the civil rights movement.

I enjoy the satisfaction of having been part of the movement which rewrote a segment of the sad history of U. S. racial discrimination and gave all Americans equal civil rights.

Today, I am involved in another struggle which is at least as important as the struggle for civil rights — a struggle for equal economic opportunity that has been and will continue to be more difficult to win.

As the publisher of Black Enterprise Magazine for more than a decade, I can tell you that the future of our people and of our nation depends on the outcome of this quest. I can also tell you that it will take more than the rewriting of local laws and the winning of court battles to achieve the dream of America's founding fathers — that all Americans would be able to enjoy the equal economic opportunity to succeed or fail based on his or her ability and determination, not on his or her race, religion or national origin.

It will take full use of all of the political, economic and personal clout we have to make true equal economic opportunity a reality for all Americans. For to achieve this goal we will have to change decades of unjust tradition in the corporate world, the world of banking and finance as well as in institutions of education and government at all levels.

I did not travel to Anchorage tonight to issue a public condemnation of this nation's corporations, banks, schools or government agencies. Some of them are trying to practice equal economic opportunity in all of their affairs and are reaping the rewards of their practices. Many more are not.

I am here tonight to state the facts -not to point a finger. I hope to give an accurate picture of the intolerable price we are paying for the lack of equal economic opportunity in America today and of consequences too grim to imagine if we allow this condition to exist at its present level much longer.

But the most important message I bring tonight is one of hope, confidence and determination. If you remember anything of what I say this evening, let it be that we already have all of the economic, political and personal clout we need to make equal economic opportunity a reality for all Americans. But it will take the utmost each of us has to give to make it happen.

Here in Alaska, a state not quite 25 years old, we have a wonderful opportunity to learn from centuries of history in the 'lower 48'.

Alaska is filled not only with the unlimited

Gov. Bill Sheffield talks with
Earl Graves Summer, 1983

natural beauty and treasure of its vast natural resources. Alaska's wealth cannot be measured simply in terms of its oil reserves, timberlands, fisheries and unspoiled nature.

With its $2 billion operating budget and more than $1 billion capital budget, the State of Alaska is in a wonderful position to help minority-owned businesses grow and prosper. How? The state could make certain that five percent of all agency business goes to minority-owned businesses, and that five percent of the capital budget goes to minority-owned construction companies. If you did that, these companies could grow and begin to prosper.

The state could also refuse to do business with banks that do not make it a practice to loan capital to minority citizens and their businesses. And, this state could make certain that companies it does business with practice equal economic opportunity in all of their affairs.

This great state and city offers all of America a new frontier in economic opportunity for men and women of all races and walks of life.

In many, many cases, you share the unique opportunity to learn from the mistakes of our past and to do it right the first time around.

In a state with so many resources to be shared among only 550,000 citizens, there is no possible excuse for anyone to suffer from a lack of real economic opportunity."

Critical to realizing the vision Mr. Graves shared for Alaska with his audience that evening is fulfilling the need for a black newspaper.

Media, print or otherwise, is vital to reporting the aspirations and progress of a people.

Since the early fifties at least four newspapers were started by blacks.[14] As an enterprises that are primarily dependent on other businesses to sustain its existence, none of the papers were able to attract

PUBLICATIONS
TABLE X

PAPER	DECADE IN WHICH PUBLISHED	EDITOR/PUBLISHER
Alaska Sportlight	1950	George Anderson
Sun Reporter	1960	Jim Owens
New Horizon	1970	Alberta Jones
North Star Reporter	1980	Charles LeViege

sufficient advertisers to assure the papers' viability. This condition reflects the plight of the black business community in Alaska.

A part of the problem was that the papers had to exhibit advocacy postures. In a number of instances the need to advocate caused white advertisers to steer clear of placing ads with these papers. However, in each instance the papers did not sacrifice their integrity to survive. As such, the papers played a significant role during the period in which they were published.

As an example, the North Star Reporter was very instrumental in providing the black communities in Anchorage and Fairbanks with coverage of the relevant issues of the 1982 gubernatorial campaign.

Today the need is greater than ever for a black owned newspaper.

However, the current economic conditions in Alaska effectively prevents this need from being met. In fact, the state's two major dailies which serve an urban area of less than a quarter million people are locked in a struggle for survival. This struggle to a noticeable degree is perceived by blacks as being waged, in part, at their expense. News relating to blacks is often sensationalized, or dramatized beyond the issues being reported impact on society.

The Anchorage Daily News, under the leadership of its publisher, Jerry Grilly, and managing editor, Howard Weaver, and staff writer Larry Campbell, who is black, has been more balanced in its coverage of issues impacting the black community than has Anchorage's other daily newspaper.

Also, In spite of lukewarm support for governmental entities, a number of small businesses have survived for over twenty years.

Hank Humphries, a well respected member of the Fairbanks civic and business communities, arrived in Alaska in 1951. After getting out of the military service he worked at odd jobs, and ran a couple of nightclubs in the mid fifties to the early sixties. In 1961 he assumed ownership of Lemata Pumping and Thawing Company. He has remained in business during the good and bad economic times the Fairbanks community has experienced. He has been a strong advocate and role model for black business development.

The Malvo family, Oscar, "Buddy", and Beatrice, after arriving in Alaska in the early fifties, have operated a number of successful service operations. Emma Walker, and Carol Smith are sisters who have been self employed beauticians for over thirty years. Similarly, in Fairbanks Phil Jackson, who came to Alaska in 1955 to work as a carpenter, put up his tools and opened a barber and beauty shop. His business has been in the same location for over 26 years. Nathaniel Neal operated the skycap services at Anchorage International Airport for over 25 years.

In Fairbanks, the Taylor brothers, George and Robert, have been installing and finishing concrete for over 25 years. Ellis "Sarge" Murray, after retiring from the military ran a successful painting company.

Like the Taylor brothers, Charles Hudson has laid a lot of concrete over the years. Chuck Ferrell, Charles Smith and Tommie Cleveland have maintained excavating operations for over two decades. However, for the most part the businesses have been family run enterprises

Walt Burks, arrived in Alaska in 1958. He was joined by his wife, Elizabeth, a year later. During an interview, he asked that the tape recorder be turned off. This accomplished, he made a confession in front of his wife for the first time in nearly thirty years. He stated, "When I told everyone I was going to Alaska for a vacation, I had no intention of returning. As it turned out, the reason he wanted the tape recorder turned off, he didn't know what his wife's reaction would be to his confession. She only smiled a knowing smile about the way his vacation had turned out for them. He started out as a barber, and later worked for 16 years as a postal worker, while he and his wife built the family business. Today the business employs nearly three dozen workers. Things must be going okay, for they departed the interview in a new top of the line Mercedes Benz.

One service business which has enjoyed a considerable measure of success for much of the past decade has been Wilsyk, Inc. At various times the company has employed up to five hundred employees. The firm, Wilsyk, Inc., was founded in 1978 by Jim Williams, and Willie Sykes, who came to Alaska as enlisted personnel in the U. S. Air Force.

In a business report published at the end of the 3rd quarter of 1987, their firm was listed as one of the top fifty employers in the state.

Along with the LeViege family who experienced success in the paint business, Wilsyk, represents the two entities that own significant commercial structures in Alaska.

Tommie Bishop, in addition to his duties as a supervisor with Northwest Airlines, has built a successful real estate practice.

However, the primary source for income for

blacks in Alaska remains wages earned as employees. Black family income, due to professional positions held in the energy industry, employment with school systems, retired military personnel working in second career jobs provide black families with a statistical standard of living higher than our counterparts in the contiguous states.

As Table XI indicates one in every nine black families in Alaska earn in excess of $50,000. Nationally, only two in every hundred black families earn in excess of $50,000.

Thus, as discussed the main challenges to socio/economic progress for blacks in Alaska remains overcoming disparate state employment statistics and gaining a piece of the public contracting pie which sustains a tremendous number of businesses.

In July of 1980[13], Congressman Parren Mitchell asked participants in the hearings, he along with his staff counsel, Major Clark, were conducting, what they would recommend to improve the minority business situation in Alaska. One respondent stated, "I recommend that it be recognized that there has been a black presence in Alaska for over 100 years. I recommend that this longevity be an entitlement to have our aspirations realized and our frustrations minimized. I recommend that wise men and women provide the understanding that all our destinies as personified in Alaska's destiny are inseparable. I recommend that blind bigots of this world be blessed with vision to see that, come what may, black folks are here to stay. I recommend that while racists of this world build walls to constrain our progress, that our minority contractors construct steps for our success. I recommend that if matters not how straight the gate, how charged with punishment the scrolls, we must be the masters of our faiths and the captains of our unconquerable souls,' Thank you." The need this statement reflects is as true today as it was seven years ago.

Pictured, George Harrison, Pres. Harrison Construction Co., Andonia Harrison, past Pres. of Anchorage, Branch NAACP, Jim Williams, Wilsyk, Inc., Senator Frank Murkowski, and Willie Sykes, Wilsyk, Inc., Washington, D.C. 1982.

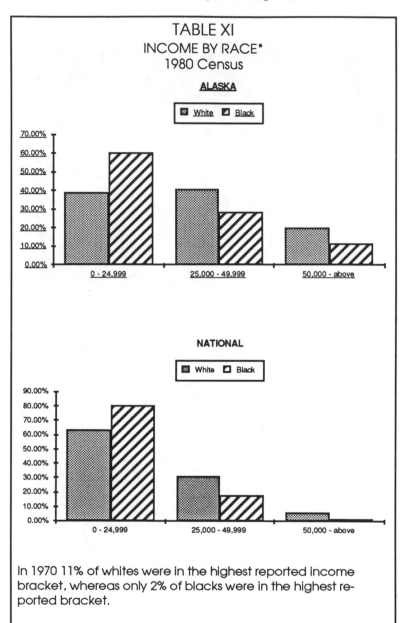

TABLE XI
INCOME BY RACE*
1980 Census

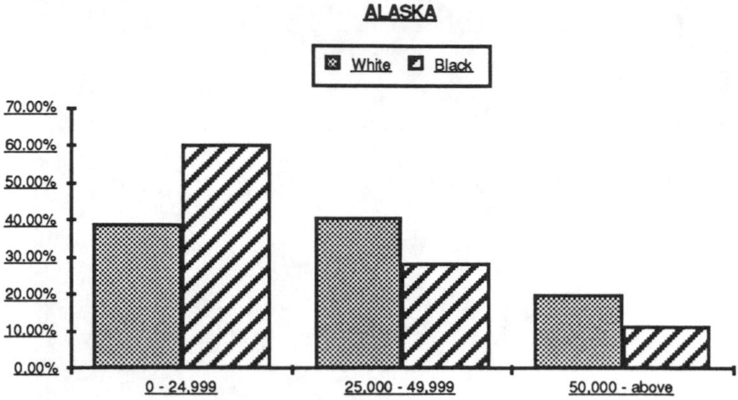

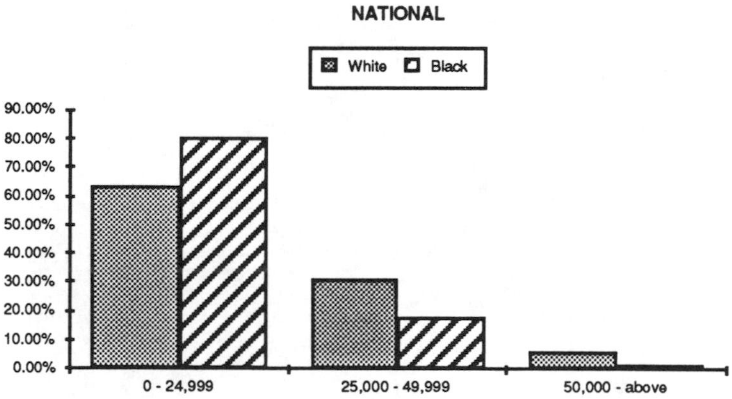

In 1970 11% of whites were in the highest reported income bracket, whereas only 2% of blacks were in the highest reported bracket.

* Not adjested for cost of living differential between Alaska and contiguous states.

1. This section was amended by the voters on August 22, 1972 with an effective date of October 14, 1972. The amendment added the word "sex" to the section. enforce Article 1, Section 3 of the Constitution.
2. Governor of Alaska from December, 1974 - December, 1982.
3. Barry Best was one of the first black appointees in the Sheffield Administration. Bill Sheffield served as Governor of the State of Alaska from December, 1982 - December, 1986.
4. H.R.C. C-78-1212-372-6.
5. A.C.N. 25-4250-86-5, April 15, 1986.
6. The ten percent set aside provision of this law was challenged all the way to the Supreme Court. In 1980 the court in the Fullilove vs Klugtznick ruled the provision constitutional. No challenges were made to the 1982 Act.
7. See Chapter X, for a discussion about this group.
8. A 800 mile 48" oil pipeline that runs from Prudhoe Bay in northernmost Alaska to the port city of Valdez, Alaska.
9. Congressman Mitchell served in the U. S. Congress from 1970-1985. From 1982-1986 he served as Chairman of the House's Small Business Committee. Recognized as the nation's foremost public authority on minority and small business development. Congresswomen Braithwaite served from 1972 to 1980.
10. For more discussion of the testimony provided by the Caucus, refer to Chapter X.
11. Hameed Ahmad, Frank Austin, Fred Johnson, Louis Overstreet, George Taylor, Sterling Taylor (no relation), and Bob Walker.

12. See Chapter X, Table XX for a list.
13. Task Force on Minority Enterprise of the Subcommittee on General Oversight and Minority Enterprise of the Committee on Small Business, House of Representatives, 96th Congress, Second Session, Anchorage, Alaska, July 16 and 17, 1980.

CHAPTER IX
CRIME, JUSTICE

Unfortunately, Alaska appears intent on addressing the issues of crime and justice in ways that are similar to that being employed in other states, with the same ineffective results.

The prevailing wisdom in the way to fight crime seems to be to allocate more money to the criminal justice system. Increasing amounts of public funds are being budgeted to hire more police, prosecutors, judges and build more prisons with the false expectation that it will buy more security for the citizenry. One could argue rather effectively that if this was the correct approach, would crime be constantly on the increase?

Currently, state government is primarily dependent on one source of revenue to fund its operations. As indicated earlier, the oil industry provides upwards of 85 percent of the state's revenue. World events since the early seventies clearly indicate our nation, and particularly its energy producing states, are at the mercy of people external to our borders. Given that world oil prices can be depressed through manipulation of production quotas, when this occurs energy states in America suffer a disproportionate impact. This creates the situation where public fiscal planning becomes an annual exercise in futility.

As long as this condition is allowed to exist, there will be tremendous political competition in Alaska for available public dollars to fund services. Politically astute elected officials and interest groups possessed with blind zeal, have little difficulty in creating the pretense that buying security from crime is a budget priority and the problem can be solved by spending more money on police, prosecutors, and prisons. In such an emotionally charged climate of fear, there exists little likelihood that serious consideration will be given to exploring alternative and more cost effective ways of reducing crime. Thus, the question of how money could be allocated differently to combat crime will go unanswered.

Compounding the condition is that blacks are over represented in arrest and conviction statistics, while at the same time are more likely to be the victims of crime. This results in a dilemma for blacks in that it is in our self interest to support effective crime preventative measures, yet remain vigilant against the potential of the system blaming the victims of crime.

As implied earlier, the uncertainty of an unstable economy notwithstanding, criminal activity causes more anxiety in most of us than any other public issue.

Today one out of every 600 Americans is under lock and key. The only two nations in the world that have a higher percentage of its people locked up than the United States are the Soviet Union and South Africa. This fact of American life supports a climate for blaming the victims of crimes and have potentially grave consequences for the not to distant future if the phenomenon of the past decade and a half manifests itself in the times to come. Crime statistics show that America's prison population more than doubled between the years of 1970 and 1984.

This fear of crime is leading towards social isolation. Without interaction our social solidarity, which is essential for the development of a sense of social well being, is often damaged beyond repair. World history is replete with examples of what happens when a group of people can be socially isolated.

Police departments can be unwitting or active participants in furthering social isolation. The attitudes exhibited by police officers often gives rise to the enmity that exits between blacks and law enforcement officials.

The relationship often results from a problem of perception. This problem must be addressed by both sides in a forthright manner if relations are to improve.

Ideally, one would like to believe the mission of the police department is to protect and patrol our communities. However, the perception in the black community is that the police are in our community to control us. Crucial to developing better relations is understanding the difference between patrolling a community and controlling a community.

Patrolling a community has a positive connotation and implies a public servant has an understanding that his or her mission is to insure a safe environment in which citizens are free to come and go, based on a presumption of innocence. Alternately, controlling a community has a negative connotation and implies public servants' actions toward the citizens are based on a presumption of guilt. When normally law abiding black citizens are routinely stopped by the police, far too often the interactions deteriorate to disrespectful exchanges which foster mistrust and animosity.

The root causes of the problems in Alaska are lack of cultural/racial awareness, small percentages of blacks and other minorities in policy making positions in the criminal justice system, disparity in bail bond requirements, or sentencing, and the use of deadly force.

In the fall of 1982 a long time Alaskan female lawyer, who is black, Mahala Dickerson, spoke out about the perception that a number of officers are psychologically unfit to serve in public trust capacities and called for the establishment of a citizen's review board. As a result of her outspokenness, the police employees association filed a frivolous suit. Many sensed this action was a tactic designed to scare off the public from supporting efforts that would lead to establishing a citizens' review board to require psychological testing for all officers.

It should be noted the suit was subsequently dropped, and the Anchorage Police Department now requires psychological screening for new officers. A citizens review board has yet to be established.

Unfortunately, until administrators are willing to talk about the problems with concerned citizens, and officers are willing to accept training that will increase their level of cultural/racial awareness, which will allow them to differentiate between the criminal and the victim, the problems will continue to exist.

It is felt the forgoing supports the assertion that blacks' experience with the justice system in Alaska frequently parallels that in evidence in the contiguous states.

As alluded to, employment opportunities within the system are limited. The lack of opportunity is especially acute for black males in the Anchorage Police Department and the State Judicial System.

The problem stems from the general population's willingness to conclude that a police department is doing a good job when it reduces levels of crime.

While the general population may be willing to

make such a simplistic correlation, it is not in the best interests of the black community to do likewise. It is incumbent on us to seek to broaden the criteria by which police departments are judged because of the existence of the conditions herein discussed.

If we accept the non-race specific criteria that quality leadership and effective policy setting as being common to all good organizations, then the question becomes: How can these elements be transmuted in order to make a determination whether a specific organization is doing a good job?

The chief of police of Madison, Wis., David Couper, in a study titled, How To Rate Your Local Police Department, that was completed in the early eighties, outlined the need to develop better standards for rating police departments. The study was commissioned by the Police Executives Research Forum (PERF), headquartered in our nation's capital.

Chief Couper suggested rating a police department should include assessing the personal integrity, courteousness, physical fitness of officers and their restraint in the use of force. Determine whether they obey the law while enforcing the law and the willingness of police administrators to support the prosecution of officers who violate the law in carrying out their duties.

Additionally, the conditions that exist in Anchorage would suggest that a criterion for measuring the effectiveness of its personnel promotion policy should also be utilized.

In the history of the Anchorage Police Department only two blacks have received promotions. These promotions came after a 2 million dollar suit was filed by a black female warrant officer who had been with the department for over 13 years in March, 1983.

The suit and promotions were subsequent to a former black state trooper, Ed Rhodes being appointed as Deputy Chief of Police for Administration. Almost immediately after being appointed to the position, over the objections of a bitterly divided Municipal Assembly which confirms appointments made by the Mayor, he was stopped for an alleged speeding incident by a junior grade officer. In spite of the fact the Deputy Chief brought to the job an outstanding 15 year service record with the state troopers, the traffic incident has limited his effectiveness within the department to promote reform. He was also passed over for consideration as appointment to Chief in late 1986. The black community hoped he would have been able to change the promotion policy within the department.

Currently promotion in the department is based on passing a written test and an oral interview. This criteria represent a strange bases for granting promotion. To become a police officer only minimum schooling and little training is required. These points of contention aside, the question that comes to mind is what profession, once a person gains entry, uses as a sole criterion for gaining advancement in the profession test taking? In professional politics this certainly is not the case. Nor is it the case in other professions. In the private sector, the more equitable standard of measuring the ability of a person to perform job related tasks in a productive manner is used as a basis to grant promotion.

In early 1983 eight community organizations coordinated a well attended conference on Community Involvement in Crime Prevention. During a work session, a police department administrator was asked the question, "Given that police officers are compensated at a rate of several thousands of dollars or more each month, what standards do administrators use to measure productivity?" Unbelievably he made some reference to the fact that the neatness of the reports turned in by an officer was a significant measure of productivity.

This response would seem to indicate the thought apparently never occurred to him that a more relevant standard would be the number of arrests made by an officer that lead to a conviction.

Implementing such a productivity standard in Anchorage would reduce the number of arrests made to merely harass citizens. This will improve police community relations. Relevant productivity measures used in concert with other criteria that reflect the quality of performance of job-related tasks could possibly lead to the much needed promotion of deserving black officers in the police department.

Comparisons of employee profile studies of the state judicial system for the years of 1983 and 1986[1] illustrate the depth of the problem at the state level.

The problem was raised for the public's view in late 1983 by the Alaska Black Caucus. The Caucus has sustained a decade long commitment to raising issues for consideration by the state's administrative and legislative branches of government. In a December, 1983 position paper the Caucus stated, "During the past several years the State Judicial System appears to have effectively eliminated the disparities, based on race, that existed in the sentencing of offenders. While we want to recognize this accomplishment, we also feel obligated to comment on the serious underutilization of minorities in professional, magistrate and judgeship positions in the Judicial System. Of the over 600 court system positions authorized under the current state budget, we find few minorities in the positions referred to above. For example, the majority of black Alaskans reside in the Third Judicial District. However, not one of the many magistrate positions in the District is filled by a black. We are encouraged by the Governor's recent decisions to increase the utilization of the multiple certificate approach to increase minority hire. How-

TABLE XII
STATE OF ALASKA
JUDICIAL SYSTEM (EMPLOYMENT)

1983

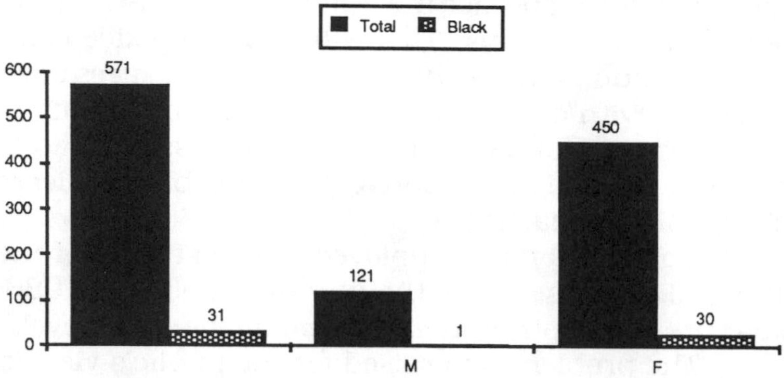

1986

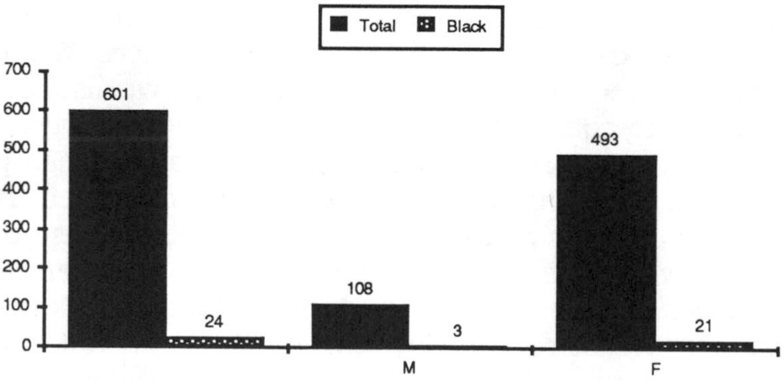

TABLE XIII
STATE OF ALASKA
JUDICIAL SYSTEM (COMPENSATION)

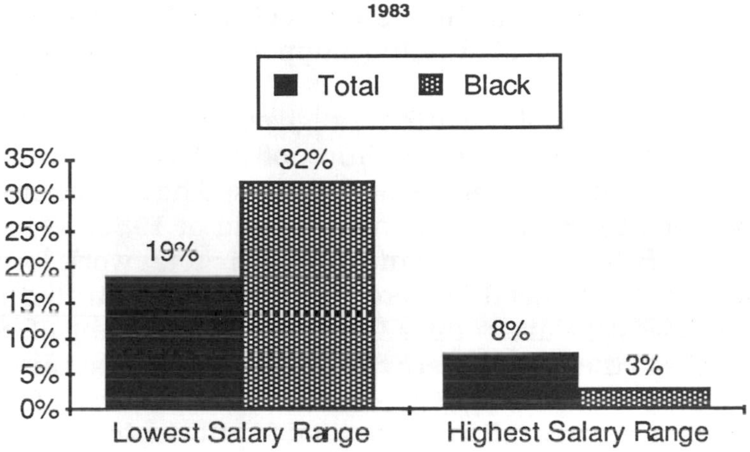

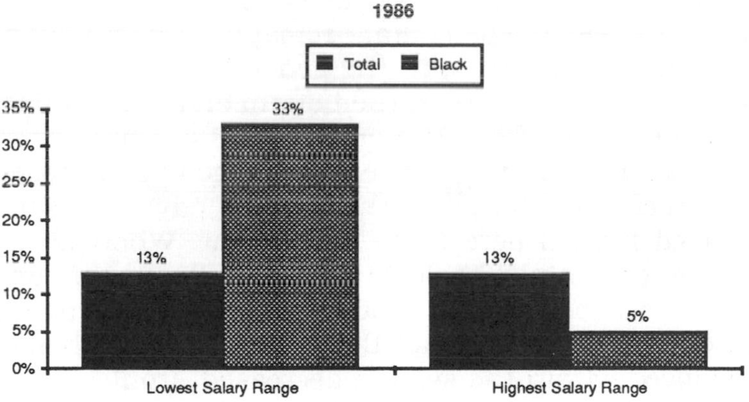

ever, we feel that the Judicial System is a special case and urge the Legislature to request an audit the minority utilization in the Judicial System. The Legislature should be prepared to join the Governor in recommending special actions to correct any inequities found. We feel that the system is clearly in jeopardy of losing any federal funding support that we now receive."

In spite of the attention given to the problem in December, 1983, the condition of underutilization of blacks in the judicial system appears to have worsened between the end of 1983 and the end of 1986.

Blacks as a percentage of their total work force within the Judicial System remained concentrated in the lowest salary ranges.[2] In 1983, 32 percent of all blacks in the system were relegated to the lowest range, as compared to only 19 percent for all employees. When blacks are removed from the total for all employees, the percentage drops to 16 percent. Stated differently only 1 out of 6 non-black employees within the Judicial System are in the lowest range. For blacks, 1 in every 3 are located in the lowest pay category.

In 1986 the percentage remained essentially the same (33%). Whereas, in the general population, the percentage of workers at the bottom end of the salary scale decreased from 19 percent to 13 percent.

Correspondingly, the percentage of all employees receiving salaries in the highest pay ranges increased from 8 percent to 13 percent. Whereas, for blacks it remained basically the same 3 percent compared to 5 percent in 1986. The small difference is accounted for by the fact the total number of blacks employed within the system decreased. Ironically the only black reported in the highest salary range for the two reporting periods is a black female who is serving in the capacity of Personnel Director.

In an effort to correct this imbalance, especially

in the higher pay ranges of which a good percentage can be appointed by the Governor when vacancies occur, blacks have helped to elect successive candidates to the Office of the Governor with a promise for a positive change. Governor Bill Sheffield, who did not win election to a second term, did not address the problem. Governor Cowper, who took office in December, 1986, has to date not addressed the problem

Two studies completed by the Alaska Judicial Council in the 1970's revealed the fact minority offenders were not being treated in a manner consistent with their majority counterparts.

The first study to be completed, which was funded in 1974 by a grant from the United States Justice Department, Law Enforcement Assistance Administration, dealt with a review of the bail process in the state. The study was entitled, Bail In Anchorage, A Description of the Process and Summary of Statistical Data for 1973. While the data generated in the study is nearly a decade and a half old, to this day, there remains strong suspicions in the black community that the problem is still in existence. Adding to the suspicion is the fact no follow-up study was ever undertaken.

The study revealed the fact crimes committed by blacks were concentrated in the statistical categories of violence and drug related offenses.[3]

Also, the study revealed the condition that blacks were more than three times as likely, 8.5 percent to 2.5 percent, than whites to remain incarcerated for bailable offenses.[4] It should be noted this inequity is consistent with the findings to be discussed related to the length of sentences blacks received as compared to whites.

The study that revealed the disparity in sentencing was completed in October of 1979 and covered the period from August, 1974 to August, 1976. The study

TABLE XIV — SENTENCE DISTRIBUTION BY RACE (1974-1976)

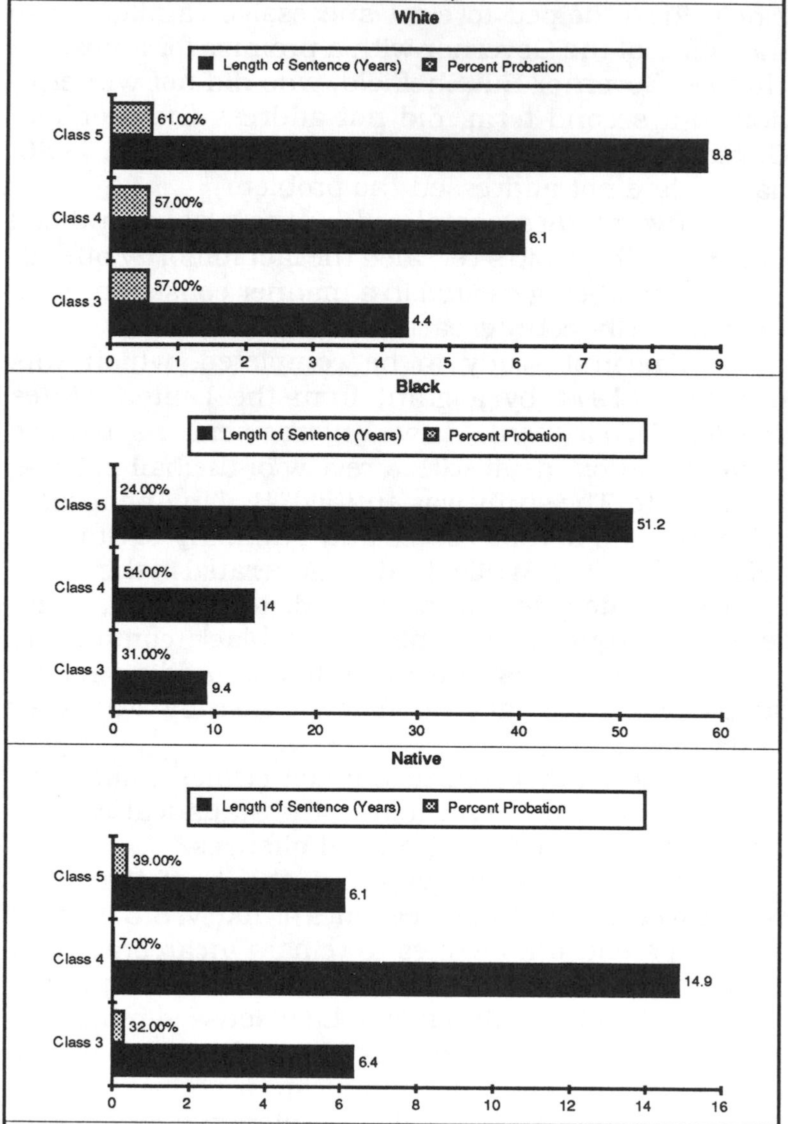

CLASS 3 - Burglary, Larceny, Receiving
CLASS 4 - Fraud, Forgery, Embezzlement
CLASS 5 - Drug Offenses

entitled, Interim Report of the Alaska Judicial Disparity in Sentencing.

The study revealed that blacks were receiving sentences up to six times that of whites for drug related offenses.[5] Also, six out of every ten whites were placed on probation. Whereas, for blacks only one in four were granted probationary status.

When the study's findings were made public in late 1979, it was accompanied by predictable levels of political embarrassment for the State's Judicial System and community outrage. Jay Rabinowitz, Chief Justice of the State's Supreme Court, after the release of the study, issued this statement, "Racism is an insidious phenomenon. I can well appreciate the concern, if not rage, of affected minorities who have suffered from various ways in which racial bias can manifest itself." He also initiated several programs in response to the Council's report.

He required the Judicial Council to annually monitor sentences in Superior and District Courts.

Established a Sentencing Guidelines Committee comprised of judges, lawyers, and Native, and minority representatives to perform a system wide study of the criminal justice system.

Mandated that during the annual judicial conference, programs will be conducted that increase the cultural and sociological awareness of judges.[6]

The Council issued a follow-up study in 1982/83, for the reporting period of 1980, that concluded disparity in sentencing had been eliminated. The elimination of the disparity was accomplished by sentencing whites to longer sentences, not be reducing the sentences issued to blacks. Also, a study released by the Alaska Judicial Council in March, 1987[7] concluded that "racial disparities in sentencing had disappeared by 1980 and did not recur in 1984 sentences."

The issue of reviewing the cases of blacks who

TABLE XV
RACE AND CRIME CATEGORIES (1973)

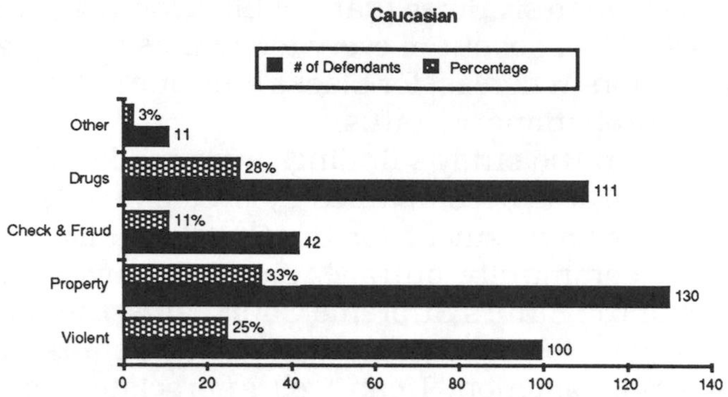

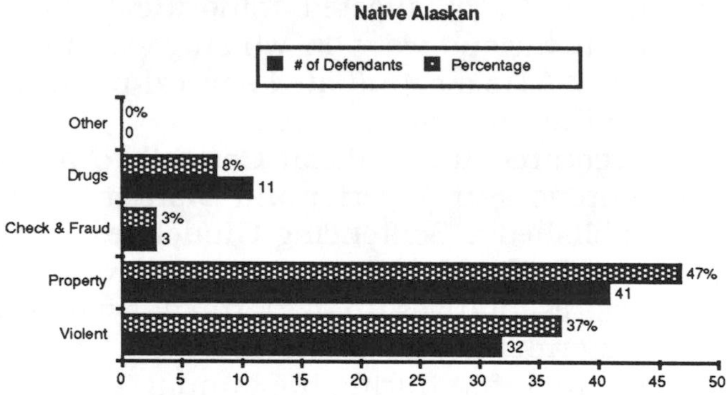

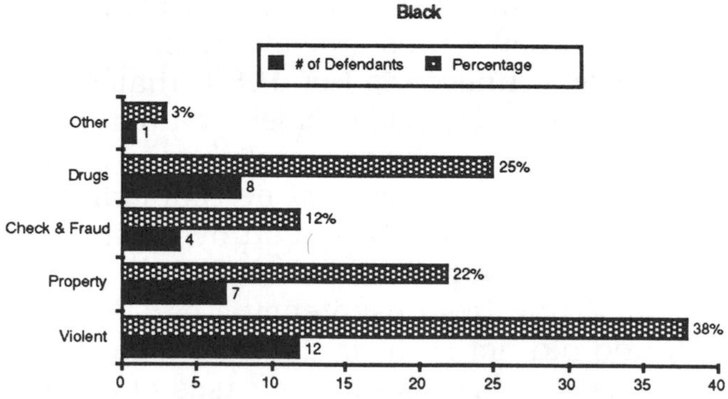

TABLE XV (con't)
RACE AND CRIME CATEGORIES (1973) (con't)

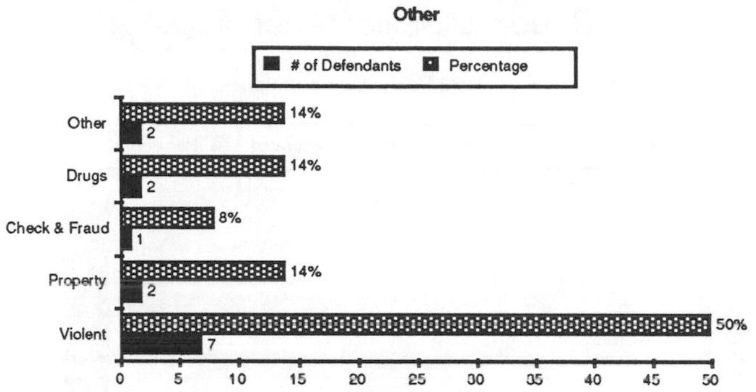

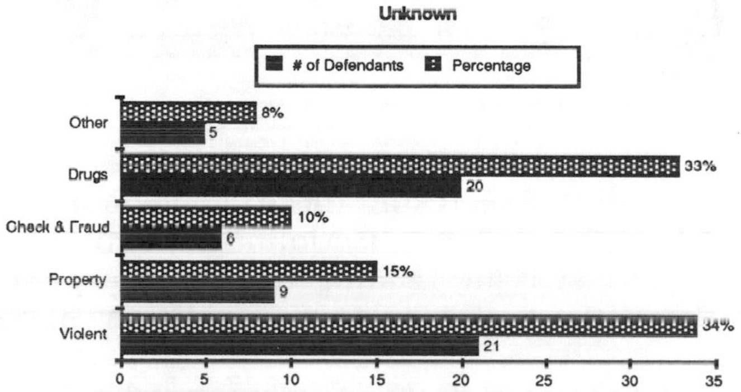

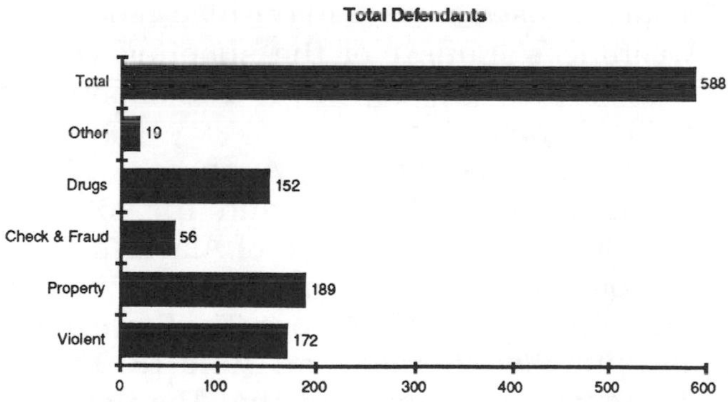

TABLE XVI
DEFENDANTS REMAINING IN CUSTODY
THROUGHOUT THE PROCESS
3rd Judicial District (Anchorage)

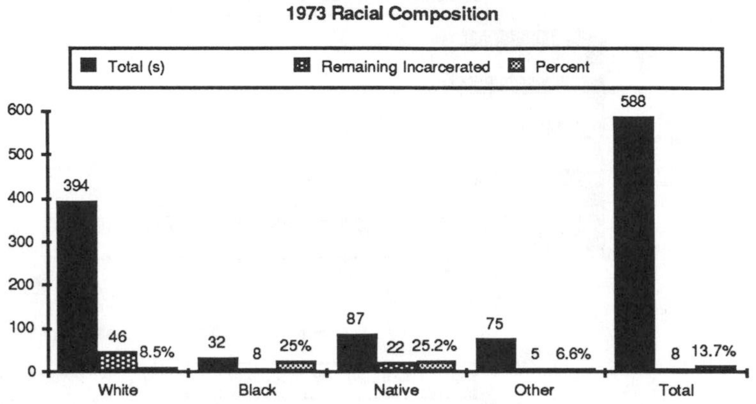

received harsher sentences has never addressed by the judicial system. As a result, these offenders have been forced to serve out their discriminatory sentences.

The last issue relating to blacks' experiences with the justice system in Alaska is the use of deadly force.

The shooting death of an unarmed black man, Phillip Moore, on January 27, 1979, by an Alaskan State Trooper, caused outrage in the black community.

A coroner's inquest of the shooting was conducted on February 14, 15, 1979. The shooting was ruled justifiable homicide.

Representatives of the Anchorage Branch, NAACP, Alaska Black Caucus, and the Ministerial Alliance requested that the State of Alaska's Department of Public Safety investigate the circumstances surrounding the death of Mr. Moore. The State honored the request and filed its report on June 18, 1979.[8]

The report recommended that the use of firearms policy be reviewed and revised. The policy was revised to include additional training for officers in February, 1981. The Anchorage Police Department also revised its firearms policy shortly thereafter.

History should note, it took a tragic death before the system was willing to example how and when it could or should use deadly force.

1. See Table XII
2. See Table XIII
3. See Table XV
4. See Table XVI
5. See Table XIV
6. The first program was held in the summer of 1980 in Sitka, Alaska and was conducted by Bob Lamb of the U. S. Justice Department. Mr. Lamb is a nationally known crisis intervener who was serving as Northwest Regional Director of the Justice Department's Community Relations Services.
7. Alaska Felony Sentences: 1984, March, 1987. (The report was accompanied by a critical comment regarding the Department of Public Safety's shooting policy.)
8. Report on the Shooting Death of Phillip J. Moore, State of Alaska, Department of Public Safety, and Department of Law.

CHAPTER X
ORGANIZATIONS/ACTIVISTS/VOLUNTEERS

In response to a social need initially and later, civic, educational, political, and economic needs a number of groups were formed.

The Alaska State Association of Colored Women's Clubs is an association of six social clubs, several of which were started in the fifties. This is the group with the longest continuous history of organized activities. The association is federated with a parent national organization. It was the first Alaskan group to host its organization's national convention. Over five hundred conferees and family members journeyed to Alaska in August of 1982 to participate in the convention.

The Anchorage Branch, NAACP, came into being in 1951,[1] and the Fairbanks Branch in 1953 in response to the need to address the civil rights issues of the day. Two National Executive Secretaries of the NAACP, Roy Wilkins and Ben Hooks, have visited Alaska on two separate occasions to access conditions in Alaska. The local branches over the years have

Pat Berkley addressing a session of the National Convention of the National Association of Colored Women's Clubs, Anchorage, August, 1982.

TABLE XVII
HISTORICAL LIST
ANCHORGE BRANCH, NAACP PRESIDENTS

NAME	YEARS SERVED
John W. Thomas	1951 - 1952
Clarence Coleman	1953 - 1960
Clarence Coleman	1961 - 1964
Blanch McSmith	1960
Blanch McSmith	1965 - 1969
Cal Williams	1969 - 1970
Alonzo Patterson	1971 1972
John Parks	1973
Jean Reynolds	1973 - 1974
Robert Kemp	1975 - 1980
Edward J. Wesley	1981 - 1982
Andonia Harrison	1983 - 1986

successfully challenged a number of civil injustices. Under successive terms as Branch President, Ed Wesley, and Andonia Harrison's voter registration drives have had a measurable impact on Alaska's historically close elections. The governor's race in 1982 was decided by less than 250 votes, and the 1984 Anchorage mayorol race was decided by less than 210 votes.

However, the Branch's finest hour as noted in Chapter VIII is generally acknowledged to be the successful picket it conducted in August, 1962.

Sorority and fraternal groups were organized to

provide community services, and promote educational excellence among black youths. Also, these groups have been actively engaged in providing financial support for students going on to college. Delta Sigma Theta was the first sorority to become active in the educational affairs of our state. The group received its charter in June, 1959. In September of 1978 Omega Psi Phi became the first fraternity to receive its charter. Other greek organizations have also been granted state charters.

In the mid to late seventies three groups came upon the scene to address political and economic issues. The groups are the Alaska Black Caucus formed in December, 1975,[2] the Greater Fairbanks Black Caucus formed in December, 1978, and the Alaska Black Leadership Conference formed in early 1979.[3]

The Alaska Black Caucus was started by 35 people, primarily concerned with promoting employment and contracting opportunities on the 48" oil pipeline that was being constructed at the time. Since its formation, the group's membership has expanded. As a result of the issues the group has championed, twenty percent of its membership is now comprised of non-black Alaskans.

The group has been at the forefront in promoting political and economic change. It incorporated into its strategy for bringing about change a networking concept with national leaders utilizing several forums.[4]

In December of 1979 the Caucus and Congressmen Mitchell coordinated responses to regulations that were being developed to govern the development of a gas line.

In a letter to the Caucus,[5] Congressman Parren Mitchell, stated in part, "I am in receipt of your response to the proposed ANGTN EEO Requirements.[6] Thank you very much. By now, you should have

JoAnn Overstreet, on behalf of Delta Sigma Theta Sorority, greeting writer, noted screen and stage performer, Ruby Dee, who is an honorary Delta, during a visit to Alaska in the Summer of 1982.

TABLE XVIII
HISTORY OF OFFICERS
ALASKA BLACK CAUCUS

OFFICE	NAME	YEARS SERVED
CHAIRPERSONS	Louie Overstreet	1977 - 1978
	Sterling Taylor	1978 - 1982
	Fred Johnson	1982 - 1985
	Bettye Davis	1985 - present
PRESIDENTS	Leroy Williams	1975 - 1978
	Louie Overstreet	1978 - 1985
	Vertis Williams	1985 - 1986
	Rex Butler	1986
	Sonya LaMarr	1986 - present
VICE PRESIDENTS	John Alexander	1975 - 1976
	Ed Moses	1976 - 1978
	Vertis Williams	1978 - 1985
	Cynthia Batts	1986 - present
SECRETARIES	Dixie Hudish	1975 - 1976
	Marlene Boderick	1976 - 1977
	Yvonne Richardson	1978 - 1980
	Eleanor Andrews	1980 - 1981
	Virginia Arnold	1981 - 1982
	Mildred Townsend	1982 - 1984
	Cynthia Batts	1984 - 1986
	Sonya Davis	1986 - present
TREASURERS	Zella Boseman	1975 - 1976
	Hameed Ahmad	1978 - 1984
	Althea Anderson	1984 - 1985
	Pat Berkley	1985 - present

FOUNDING BOARD DIRECTORS
OF THE
GREATER FAIRBANKS BLACK CAUCUS

William Allen	Hank Humphrey	Barry Best
J. P. Jones	Jack Caldwell, Sr.	Vander Pearson
Renee Chaney	George Taylor	Glayds Hamilton

TABLE XIX
ALASKA BLACK LEADERSHIP CONFERENCE
"CONCERNED, COMMITTED, INVOLVED AND UNITED"

ANCHORAGE

A.I.M.
Alaska Black Caucus
ASACWC
Alaska Women Civic and Social Clubs
Alpha Phi Alpha Fraternity, Alaska Chapter
Black Coalition
Delta Sigma Theta Sorority, Alaska Chapter
Ministerial Alliance
Mothers for Christian Fellowship
NAACP, Anchorage Branch
Omega Psi Phi Fraternity, Alaska Chapter

FAIRBANKS

Acacia Chapter No. 5, OES
Alaska Associates
American Negro Enterprises
Arctic Lodge No. 7, F and AM
Borealis Chapter No. 2, OES
Enriched Corporation
Greater Fairbanks Black Caucus
Midnight Sun Lodge No. 3, F and AM
Ministerial Alliance
NAACP, Fairbanks, Branch

received my recent news release on the ANGTA EEO requirements. Needless to say, I was not pleased with the proposed regulations. It was for this reason that I suggested eight changes in these regulations."

The final regulations for the project were adopted on May 9, 1980. In a press release accompanying the adoption of the rules issued by the Office of the Federal Inspector stated in part, "These rules were devised to carry out the intent of the Congress, to assure that minorities and minority business enterprises receive opportunities, to the maximum extent

TABLE XX
PARTICIPANTS IN
ALASKA BLACK CAUCUS
FORUMS

YEAR	PARTICIPANT	PROFESSION
1976	Jay Hammond	Governor, Alaska
1977	Lowell Thomas[1]	Lt. Governor, Alaska
	Dick Gregory	Comedian, Activist
1978	Kenneth Gibson	Mayor, Newark, New Jersey
1979	Parren Mitchell	Congressman, Maryland
	Terry Miller	Lt. Governor, Alaska
1980	Mike Gravel	U. S. Senator, Alaska
	Louis Martin	Special Assistant to President Jimmy Carter
	Rosalind Cash	Movie Actress
1981	Max Robinson	ABC-TV, Network News Anchor
	Claude Perkins	Superintendent Schools, Clark County, Nevada
	Ossie Davis	Playwright, Actor
	Ruby Dee	Actress, Broadway Performer
	Alex Haley	Author, "Roots"
1982	Tony Knowles	Mayor, Anchorage, Alaska
	Tony Brown	T.V. and Syndicated Journalist
	Thelma Duggin	Special Assistant to President Ronald Reagan
	Calvin Rolark	Publisher, Washington Informer

possible, to participate in the construction, operation and maintenance of the natural gas pipeline system. Our objective is to deliver the results intended by these regulations, which is to substantially improve minority and female participation in this project. We will concentrate on setting aggressive goals, and meeting them, as opposed to the generation of unnecessary paperwork."

TABLE XX
PARTICIPANTS IN
ALASKA BLACK CAUCUS
FORUMS (con't)

YEAR	PARTICIPANT	PROFESSION
1983	Earl Graves	Publisher, Black Enterprise Magazine
	Coy Eklund	Chairman, Equitable Life
	Willie Tyler & "Lester"	Entertainer, T.V. Personality
	Tyree Bloomfield	Chief of Police, Dayton, Ohio
1984	Walt Fauntroy	Congressman, District of Columbia
	Constance Baker Motley	Federal Judge
	Susan Taylor	Editor-In-Chief, Essence Magazine
	Suzette Charles	Miss America
1985	Frank Murkowski	U. S. Senator, Alaska
	"Mickey" Leland	Congressman, Texas
	Micki Grant	Playwright, Lyricist
1986	Bill Sheffield	Governor, Alaska
	Shirley Chisholm	Congresswoman, New York

1. After giving a speech before the Alaska Black Caucus on November 24, 1977 where he stated for the record that inter-racial marriages go against the laws of nature, he was dropped as a running mate of Jay Hammond for a second term. Governor Hammond's wife is an Alaskan Native. Excerpts from the speech were reported in the November 25, 1977 edition of the Anchorage Times

In 1979 dollars, the project was estimated to cost $20 billion to construct. When the pipeline is finally constructed, the efforts of a Congressman from Maryland and that of an Anchorage based organization should result in a "piece of the action" going to companies who may not have heard of the people most directly responsible for the input that lead to the modification of the rules which governed its development.

Susan Taylor, Editor-in-Chief, Essence Magazine, pictured in front of Portage Glacier while visiting Alaska in 1984

Alex Haley, author of Roots, with Anchorage youth and Sterling Taylor during his visit to alaska in 1980.

Calvin Rolark, publisher of the Washington Informer, addressing a gathering in Alaska in the summer of 1982.

Also during this period of time the Caucus sent lobbying teams to the nation's capital to speak to legislation that was pending before Congress.

The Caucus' position of energy development in Alaska was entered into the Congressional Record by Congressman, Don Young[7] The position was in opposition to actions being proposed by Congresspersons in support of the environmental lobby. A number of environmental groups were lobbying representatives to support legislation that would effectively "lock up" Alaska to energy and hard rock mineral exploration. The position statement came under attack from a number of representatives, the most notable being Congressman John Siberling of Ohio. Ironically his family's fortune was made in the auto tire manufacturing industry. "What's all this propaganda about? What prompts the Caucus to suggest the Udall-Anderson bill will cripple our economy, bring back the gas lines, or block development of Alaska's energy potential? By designating ANWR as wilderness, the House overwhelmingly decided that this should be the last place we look for petroleum after other potential areas in Alaska have been explored and developed. That is the real burden of the Caucus' complaints, the real reason for the absurd litany of misinformation and distortions which we again are beginning to be heard here in the House and at the other end of the Capital"[8].

The basis for the need for the attack was that the Alaska Black Caucus' position was in conflict with what the liberal Congresspersons were telling members of the Congressional Black Caucus. They were attempting to convince members of the Congressional Black Caucus that their vote to "lock up" Alaska was a good trade for gaining the support of the environmental groups on the next civil rights issue to come before Congress. Thus, when the Alaska Black Caucus stated that the "lock- up of Alaska was not an environmental issue, but an economic development issue that could benefit Alaska in general." The stakes became more than a mere trading of votes, it became a basic need for black progress in Alaska. The Alaska Black Caucus was successful in gathering a measure of support from the Congressional Caucus on this issue. However, the majority of its membership sided with the liberal part of view. It is of historical importance to note that Congresswoman Shirley Chisholm provided Alaska with a crucial role in the House Rules Committee so that the state can argue its position more favorably when the bill was scheduled for floor action in the House.

Also, the issue served to provide the Alaska Black Caucus with ongoing access to the halls of Congress.

During a visit to Alaska during the summer of 1986, after she had retired from the Congress. Ms. Chisholm, the first black female to campaign as the Democratic nominee for President in 1972, gave a rousing speech befitting the title of her autobiography, "Unbought and Unbossed". In part she stated, "It's difficult for a woman to run for public office because of the inaccessibility to funds. Men still will not support women as political candidates, and they are the ones with the money." She went on to state, "A women in politics has to have one prevailing quality - audacity."

Additionally, the Caucus annually submits position papers to the state legislature of the issues of the day[9]. Its ongoing support for the oil industry to include support for a stable tax climate for the oil industry in Alaska at the time liberal democratic legislators were advocating an increase, caused another controversy.

In the early eighties, when the Caucus voiced its support for the oil industry's position on taxation, it came under attack from both liberal Democratic legislators and two community leaders.

The Caucus stated their aim has always been to support people who support them. Its statement of support which was forwarded to the legislature read in part, "The bills offer tax stability to the energy industry and benefit tax reductions to other Alaska businesses. Therefore, we feel the legislation is capable of providing an improved investment climate."

The Caucus had gathered information that revealed, on a per capita basis, the oil industry was providing more employment opportunities for blacks than was state government. Further, black community groups were not receiving grants from the state to meet public community needs. This fact existed at a time the state was issuing grants to various special interest groups at record levels.

Brian Rogers, a legislator from Fairbanks in a news article stated, "I'm appalled that an organization (Caucus) such as yours has been snowed by the biased and inflammatory advertising carried on by the oil and gas industry in our state that you would actually advocate tax relief for an industry whose shameful profit margin comes directly from the pockets of poor people." Another legislator, Vic Fischer, stated in the same article "that because of the Caucus' support for the oil industry, legislation I'm pushing for minority preference in bidding on state contracts will be held up."[10] For historical accuracy it should be noted that Senator Fischer, as well as Senator Joe Josephson, have been, in general, very supportive of female and minority rights issues.

In response to the legislators criticism, the Caucus responded in a news release that it resented the patronizing tones of the letters and public statements. The legislators' threat to hold hostage programs which represent the dreams and aspirations of an entire community borders on lunacy.

Black persons who spoke out against the Caucus on the issue were seemingly unaware that the need for blacks had shifted from being socially acceptable to the battle for economic viability.

Ted Moore, president of the Ministerial Alliance, at the time in a news article stated, "When the Caucus is talking about such subjects as oil taxes, they're speaking for themselves and not the majority of blacks." Another black, Vince Casey, who held a number of public sector jobs in the mid-seventies through the mid-eighties characterized the Caucus as wanting to identify with the party in power. "It's kind of a slave mentality."[11]

In early 1979 a group of twenty blacks, at the invitation of State Senator, Bill Summer, journeyed to the state's capital. The group activities were coordinated by the Senator's aide, Jerrold Watts. The issues that were identified as in need of address included the recently disclosed lack of employment opportunities for minorities and females in state government, no grant programs being administered by blacks, and limited representation on state boards, commissions. The group's efforts led to the formation of the Alaska Black Leadership Conference. The conference is a federation of twenty one organizations located in Fairbanks and Anchorage.

The conference's motto is "Concerned, Committed, Involved and United."

Accomplishments that can be directly traced to the conference's actions in its first year of existence include gaining appointment of a black to the Governor's Blue Ribbon Committee on Alaskan Lands, funding for a community based tutorial program for minority students, a technical assistance center for minority and female businesses, and an employment program for youths.

Over the years, a number of individuals have

Former Congresswoman, Shirley Chisholm

TABLE XXI
ALASKA BLACK CAUCUS

YEAR	POSITION PAPER STATEMENTS	
1980	Funding for Alaska Plan	Funding MBE Centers
	D.C. Voting Rights Amendment	Human Rights Commission
	Trade Mission to Africa	
1981	Education Cost	Health Care Cost
	Taxation of Oil Industry	Lifeline Utility Rate
	Location of State Offices	
1982	Financial Assistance Programs	Senate Bill 45
	Capital Investment Fund	Governor's Budget Address
1983	Representation of Board/Commissions	Transportation Planning
	State Spending	
	Contract Compliance	
1984	DOTPF's[1] Employment/ Contracting Practices	
	Credit Practices	
	Presidential Primary	
	Judicial System	
1985	Legislator's Salaries	
	House Bills 50,119,135,147 & 163	
	Funding for Education	
	DOTPF's Employment/ Contracting Practices	
1986	DOTPF's Employment/ Contracting Practices	
	EEO Policies	
	Investment in South Africa	
1987	Senate Bill 341	Human Rights Commission
	Judicial System	DOTPF's Employment / Contracting Practices

1. Department of Transportation and Public Facilities.

advocated for change to benefit the community. Many have labored without notoriety, others gained fame, all have made a difference.

John Thomas came to Anchorage from Juneau in 1941, to work for the Defense Department on the project that is now Elmendorf AFB, Alaska.

John's political and social awareness of the need for minority equality became firmly established in 1947 when he joined the Carpenter's Union. This union was instrumental in breaking union discriminatory barriers that barred blacks from bush construction projects. Open occupancy was the next area of injustice to be handled under the leadership of John. When the Anchorage Branch, NAACP was established, John became its first president. He was instrumental in the passage of the Alaska Fair Employment Practices Law which saw the establishment of the Alaska Commission on Human Rights by former Governor William Egan. In 1952, John was a candidate for the Territorial State Legislature. Although he was not elected, this was a major step forward because no other black had ever run for the state legislature.

Shortly after John passed away in 1984, the Municipality named a building in his honor.

Ben Humphries came to Alaska in the late forties. For many years he was active in organized labor, raising through the ranks to become business agent and financial secretary for the painters' union, a position he held for over twenty years.

He is very active in Democratic Party politics. He has served on a number of professional and civic boards to include the National Bank of Alaska, and as a charter Board Member of the Anchorage Equal Rights Commission.

Richard Watts came to Alaska in 1949. Today he still looks like he has the ability to accept any challenge.

"When I first came here, a black person couldn't

get a job as a clerk in a store," he says, recalling his arrival in 1949. "Education didn't mean a thing. You could have a Ph.D. but they wouldn't hire you as a teacher. About all that was open to a black was work as a janitor or a ditch digger."

He had been in Anchorage a week when he and ten other black men formed the "Young Men's Improvement Club," which was dedicated to change. They sought the cooperation of labor unions and passed out flyers on street corners to make the public aware of the situation.

"Only one printer in Anchorage, Service Printers, would print our flyers. No one else would handle them," he said.

"Housing was another problem for the black population. Agents wouldn't even talk to them about buying a home," Watts says. The first residential area in Anchorage opened to black home-buyers was in Nunaka Valley, where he first bought a home.

The fact that Anchorage has dealt with housing discrimination in a very acceptable manner, can to a considerable measure be traced to the efforts of Mr. Watts and his pioneering colleagues.

Pearl Caldwell arrived in Alaska in 1949 with her husband, since deceased. After assisting her husband with his job as a Chef for the U. S. Army for a short while, they started a construction business and constructed the first multi-family units for black civilians' use. In 1955 she helped to organize the Northern Lights Civic and Social Club and served as its president for six years.

Katherine Hebron arrived in Alaska in 1950. She opened the first black grocery store, as well as a restaurant in the Eastchester Flats' area.

In 1953 she helped to organize the Gloom Chasers Social and Charity Club. Later in the sixties she operated the Blue Note Grill on 15th Avenue just west of Ingra Street. Today she remains active in her church and a number of senior citizen groups.

Clarence Coleman's trip to Alaska was to help in the war effort in 1944. He spent 14 months building airfields in the Aleutian Chain. He returned to Alaska in May of 1951.

A recap of Clarence's development in Alaska would show a rise from a $50 a week job and a bed in a commercial bunk house to owner-operator of a company that employed as many as 150 persons.

One look at his business success and you would wonder where he found time to help the community. From his initial involvement as a member of the Anchorage Chapter of NAACP in 1951, he rose to serve his first term as president in 1953. He served in that position from 1953-1960 and 1961-1964. During those years, Anchorage saw many changes in the treatment of blacks. The NAACP was the catalyst for most of the changes. Flossie Coleman was very active in helping her husband build the business and people still talk about her membership drives for the NAACP.

Eula Cleveland arrived in Anchorage, after a trip up the Alcan Highway in April 1951. While her husband, Tommy, was working to build their construction company, she became active in community affairs. If it is true that money makes the world go around, then it might be said that Eula was the wheels of the Anchorage Branch, NAACP. She served as chairperson of its ways and means committee for over a decade. During her tenure as chairperson, the branch hosted a visit by Roy Wilkins, then the National Executive Secretary of the NAACP.

Every person alters our environment and leaves an impression of his individual worth. Mr. John Parks is certainly no exception to this rule. He came to Alaska from Monrovia, California on May 1, 1951 with 14 cents in his pocket and a hope for a better future.

John had learned carpentry, a marketable skill, from his father. Upon his arrival, he immediately went to work. Affectionately called the "Mayor of Fairview", he worked to get the streets paved in the Fairview Community by going door-to-door to get petitions signed. It worked, the streets were paved!

He is often cited as the community person most responsible for bringing public transportation to Anchorage. His one man voter registration campaigns are legendary. At 50 cents a voter, John for many years, has been able to add to his retirement income by registering voters. By speaking out on controversial issues for over 35 years, he has made a positive influence on the status of minorities in Alaska.

Nathaniel Neal came to Alaska in 1952. From the very beginning he was and to this day remains active in political, civic, and social affairs. He is probably best known for providing skycap services at the Anchorage International Airport for twenty six consecutive years, during which time he provided employment for over a thousand people. As faith would have it, the state bureaucrats in charge of airport concessions decided to put the operation out for bid, once they discovered that it was a profitable enterprise. This action was taken by the infamous Alaska Department of Transportation and Public Facilities and is consistent with its history for non-enforcement of federal laws pertaining to the utilization of minority and women businesses. While running his business, he also found time to speak out on the plight of blacks in Anchorage and was pastor of the Evergreen Temple of Church of God in Christ for nine years.

Fred and Annie Zimmerman arrived in Alaska in May, 1952. While they have run a number of successful family owned businesses to include a janitorial service company and a multi-family housing development

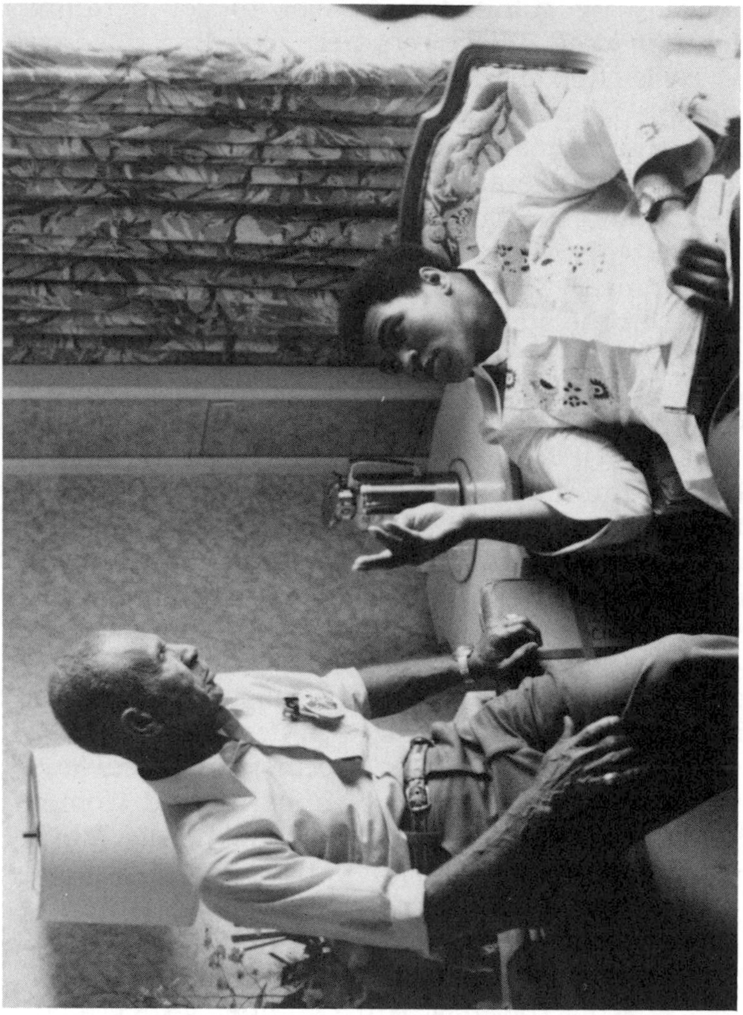

John Parks, pictured with former three time heavyweight champion, Muhammad Ali.

company, the position of respect they enjoy in the community stems from the public recognition of their years of volunteer service and leadership positions they have held in a host of civic organizations.

Joe Jackson moved to Anchorage from Los Angeles in June of 1952. He has been active in the civic and business community since the date of his arrival. His first job in Alaska was that of a carpenter. He practiced this skilled craft while studying for the real estate exam.

In 1954, Joe was licensed as the first black male real estate broker in the State of Alaska; subsequently he became the first black member of the National Real Estate Board for the State of Alaska. He was an organizing participant in the establishment of several churches. He passed away in the summer of 1987 after a long bout with cancer.

Mary Siah first moved to Fairbanks in 1953. After suffering a serious accident in 1970, she retired from her job and rehabilitated herself. After rehabilitating herself, she pursued community service and organizing activities with such zeal, that she has become a living legend. Her volunteer efforts have been duly noted, as evidenced by the numerous community service awards that cover her living room walls. She and her husband, Hollis, maintain their house and surrounding grounds in a neat and orderly fashion as would be excepted of persons who are very good at organizing activities.

The recognition she is obviously the proudest of was the honor the community and city officials bestowed upon her in 1980. A recreation center, where she has spent countless hours, was renamed in her honor.

George Taylor arrived in Anchorage, Alaska in 1953 to do construction work in the summer and tend bar in his brother's club, Lucky's Hot Spot, in the

Mary Siah of Fairbanks, Alaska

winter.

He moved to Fairbanks in 1957. During the intervening years, he has been active in church, civic, political and minority business development activities.

He is the person generally recognized as being the one most responsible for fostering and coordinating a working relationship between the black communities in Anchorage and Fairbanks for political and economic empowerment.

A number of other persons have been active in the community events of Fairbanks over the years to include school teacher, Virgie King, who is a Commissioner with the State Commission on Human Rights, and was a delegate to the 1984 Democratic Convention. Jack Caldwell, Gladys Hamilton, Callie Martin, and Annie Sloane enjoy positions of respect in the Fairbanks community.

Toby and Helen Gamble arrived in Alaska in the early fifties. Since that time, their volunteer efforts and assistance to new arrivals to Alaska have earned the honorary title of Mom and Dad to a generation of younger people.

Mahala Dickerson, in the fifties, became the first black licensed to practice law in Alaska. She has tried many lawsuits dealing with the rights of minorities and women. She has won landmark appellate decisions dealing with Worker's Compensation and condemnation issues.

Also, she is licensed to practice law in Alabama, Indiana, and before the U. S. Supreme Court. She is a past president of the National Association of Women Lawyers. One of her triplet sons, in the early eighties, won the body building title of Mr. Olympia.

Jimmie Lockhart and Willie Ratcliff are viewed as masters at attacking the status quo. Both ran successful construction businesses until the system made them pay the price for their political and commu-

Pioneer Alaskans:(l to r) Jo Elizabeth Porter(42), Pete Aiken(50), Elizabeth Banks(59), Marshall(53), Walt Burks(58 George Taylor(53), Leroy Parham(53), Phil Jackson(51) and Hank Humphries(51). Year of arrival in Alaska shown in parenthesis, indicates that combined time in Alaska totals 313 years.

nity organizing activities. Jimmie was a Republican candidate for Governor during the 1978 campaign. Willie was instrumental in organizing a group of small contractors in Fairbanks into Alaska Associates. This group was successful in getting a contract on the Trans Alaska Pipeline System to construct concrete pipeline anchors.

Charlie Mae "Pat" Berkley has been characterized by close friends as volunteer for the ages. For over thirty years she has been active in a host of social, education, and political organizations.

During her tenure as state president, the Alaska State Association of Colored Women's Clubs, it hosted its parent organization's national convention. Since its inception, she has served as Anchorage President of the Alaska Black Leadership Conference for a number of years. Under her guidance the ABLC's tutorial program has resulted in a marked improvement in the achievement of minority students.

Her tireless fund raising efforts have resulted in a number of community groups being placed on firm financial footing. In between being recognized statewide for her activities, to include being the recipient of the State of Alaska First Lady's Award for volunteer service, Eddie her husband of forty years, and she have found the time to raise six children.

Chuck Powell has managed a number of enterprises since coming to Alaska in the late fifties. However, he is most readily identified with co-founding the "Juneteenth" celebration in Alaska. At its zenith this activity attracted thousands of Alaskans to the park in downtown Anchorage.

Johnnie Gay came to Alaska from Los Angeles before statehood in 1958. After living in Fairbanks for three years, Johnnie moved to Anchorage in 1961. After witnessing many of the social, economical, and political inequities in all segments of Anchorage,

Johnnie became involved in the community. In 1967 she became chairperson of the Board of Community Action Council. This council helped to establish many community services including public transit programs for the elderly, low income housing, food stamp program, and minority employment programs.

Leroy Williams, mustered out of the military in Alaska. Shortly thereafter, he helped to found the Alaska Black Caucus and served as its first president. During his tenure in late 1977, Lt. Governor, Lowell Thomas, was extended an invitation to speak to the group to expand on his reported views about South Africa and inter-racial marriage among Alaskans. His speech was covered by the media. The Lt. Governor's views so incensed the incumbent governor, who was married to an Alaskan native, that he dropped the Lt. Governor as a running mate for a second term.

Vander Pearson, the first president of the Greater Fairbanks Black Caucus, has maintained a visible profile in the community. Through the political caucus process, he was elected as a delegate for Jesse Jackson to the Democratic National Convention held in San Francisco in July 1984.

His stand on principle, caused him to feel the scorn of Willie Hensley, a Native, who was serving as state chairman of the Democratic Party at the time. Vander, rather than compromise his values, refused to withdraw his support for a plank in the Jackson Platform that called for defense spending cuts. Also, he refused to cast a ballot for Walter Mondale after the results were known. His refusal was based on the fact that he felt qualified blacks were not given serious consideration as a running mate for Mondale. News accounts indicated that Mr. Hensley publicly called Mr. Pearson's party loyalty into question. The black community felt it was the height of hypocrisy for Hensley to question Pearson's loyalty, when a couple years earlier it was indicated that Hensley was giving consideration to running for Lieutenant Governor on a ticket headed by a Republican.

Sterling Taylor, a member of the Equitable's Hall of Fame of Insurance Agents, was a major force in the growth of the Alaska Black Caucus in the late seventies and early eighties.

Bob Kemp, was the NAACP's branch president during the late seventies. Under his leadership, in an association with several other community leaders, after the shooting of an unarmed black man by a state trooper, they were successful in getting the Alaska State Troopers and the Anchorage Police Department to revise their fire arm policies when the use of deadly force could be utilized.

Without a doubt the most unconventional, controversial, and probably the most effective, if not fully appreciated, activist of the late seventies and early eighties has been Phil Pleasant, from Yakima, Washington. His willingness, as well as the manner in which he champions community causes is the stuff that gives rise to Alaskan folklore. He was dubbed the "lone picketer" by one of his fellow activists out of respect. He does not wait for organizations, which are often vying for public acceptance to meet and reach a consensus, but instead rushes out an establishes his picket line of one to dramatize conditions. During construction of the International Terminal at the Anchorage Airport, he wrapped himself in chains which dragged along the ground as he walked back and forth in front of the site with his sign. This act served to dramatize the fact that no minority contractors or workers were involved in a multi-million dollar public construction project being managed by the infamous State Department of Transportation and Public Facilities.

Andonia Harrison, along with her husband, George, arrived in Alaska from North Carolina in the

Phil Pleasant picketing the Federal Building talking with Congressman Parren Mitchell, summer, 1980

late sixties. In the seventies their family business constructed some of the finest homes in Anchorage. Their company diversified in the eighties to become involved in commercial construction. Some of their projects include the remodeling of Alaska Air Command Inspector General Building, Spenard-McRae Road Expansion and the Anchorage International Airport Parking Garage. Also, during this period of time she served in a number of capacities with the NAACP to include two terms as its president. During her tenure, the branch hosted the appearance of the NAACP's National Executive Secretary, Ben Hooks. In late 1986, Andonia was elected to serve as chairperson for the NAACP of Region I, which consists of 9 states. This was the first time in the local branch's history that a representative from Alaska had been elected to serve in a regional capacity. Also, she has been credited by her peers for restoring a sense of ethics to the State Bar Commission as a public appointee.

Since the early eighties, Charles McGee has been considered the ambassador without portfolio in the black community. He is a master at showing up at community meetings and prescribing a course of action that invariably raises the level of intellectual discourse.

By the mid-eighties, Willie Sykes had become the most politically active lay person in the community. He has been successful in raising money and votes for a host of local and state-wide candidates.

Also, he took a leave of absence from his company to serve in an appointed capacity in state government to promote minority business development. As a private businessman, along with his partner, Jim Williams, their company has provided financial support for a number of community based groups.

He and his wife, Sandi, have three grown children, Hisa, Ken, and Gwen. All are college graduates.

Hisa and Ken have followed in their father's footsteps in community and political involvement. Gwen is working in a position with the federal government in Washington, D. C. Their youngest son, Rashid, is approaching high school age.

A number of blacks who served tours of military duty in Alaska have demonstrated a sense of community while stationed here. In the seventies it was Captain Dick Peace, Major Cal Murray, and Colonel Jim Greene who provided organizational expertise to community and religious groups. In the eighties it has been Chief Master Sergeants (Ret.), Gene Akers, and Sylvester Perry and First Sergeant Bernard Jackson who have been active in a host of community organizations and helping hand projects. The latter three all have received awards in recognition of their community service activities.

1. See Table XXII for historical listing of officers.
2. See Table XVIII, for historical list of officers or Board of Directors.
3. See Table XIX, for historical list of groups.
4. See Table XX, for listing of persons who have participated in Caucus forums.
5. Dated December 21, 1979.
6. Alaska Natural Gas Transportation Act, Section 17, Bill of Concerns submitted by the Alaska Black Caucus to Dept. of Interior, and Federal Energy Regulatory Commission, on October 2, 1979.
7. Congressional Record, October 10, 1979, "Alaska Energy".
8. Undated Anchorage Times article, circa October-November, 1979.

9. See Table XXI.
10. Fairbanks Daily News Miner, May 23, 1981.
11. Anchorage Daily News Article, January 16, 1982.

CHAPTER XI
EDUCATING A RACE

Blacks have been involved in the public school systems in Alaska in representative numbers since the early sixties. However, appointments to administrative and teaching positions at the university level continues to lag behind population figures.

Allegations of discrimination have been made about the University of Alaska for nearly a decade. However, a series of university presidents have failed to correct the problem. Also, a number of inept appointments by Governors Hammond, Sheffield and Cowper to the Board of Regents, of the University of Alaska, based more on political cronyism than ability to provide educational leadership, has been a major contributing factor to the lack of corrective steps being mandated.

The lack of employment in the state university system has been the source of constant concern since the mid seventies. The depth of the problem was first uncovered during the recruitment for a basketball coach to head up the program at the University of Alaska, Anchorage in 1977.

The Anchorage Branch, NAACP, and the Alaska Black Caucus alleged that the process was a "sham". The hand picked search committee selected a white coach whose experience had been at junior college, over a black coach, Floyd Laisure, who had a winning record at two different four year universities. The embarrassment that followed the public disclosure of the search resulted in the reform in the process for appointing search committees. Ironically the coach that was hired over Mr. Laisure was dismissed from the university for violating a number of NCAA rules governing inter-collegiate athletics. Also, an Affirmative Action Officer, James Chase, was hired for the Anchorage Campus shortly after the incident.

However, blacks have continued to experience difficulties at the university. The two most notable instances involved Welton Lawrence, and Dr. Ron Smith.

When Ron Smith, who was serving as Vice Chancellor at the time, appointed Welton Lawrence as Director of Aviation Programs at Anchorage Community College in the Fall of 1982, the appointment became a cause celebre for instructors and administrators. After serving in the position for one year, he resigned and left the campus to complete work on his doctorate. He returned to the college as an instructor in 1985.

Dr. Smith ran into difficulties when a new chancellor, Herb Lyon, was hired out of New Mexico in 1984. In spite of the fact Ron Smith had served in administrative positions with the college for six years, to include one year as acting chancellor, Lyon asked for his resignation. When Dr. Smith refused, he was reassigned. His contract was not renewed after the 1985/86 academic year. This action resulted in a lawsuit being filed against the college. The case is still pending in the Superior Court of Alaska as of the summer of 1987.

A reorganization plan for combining the administration of the four year university campus with that of the two year community college, approved in early 1987, eliminated Herb Lyon's position.

In part, Herb Lyon's departure may have been hastened by Nina Harding, a member of the college's advisory council. Her articulate support, which was befitting her law school background, of Dr. Smith was praised by the student body and reported in the newspapers.

A number of people feel that the lack of equitable opportunity, as well as the inflated cost to educate a student in the state's university system will continue to prevent its development into a quality university.

In 1984, university campuses at Fairbanks, Anchorage and Juneau had a total full-time equivalent enrollment of less than 3,600 students. Under-graduate and graduate degrees were conferred on less than 800 students.

Based on an operating budget of a quarter billion dollars, it is costing the citizens of Alaska more than $69,000 a year to maintain a full time student in the university system.

The average cost to graduate a student, reached by dividing the annual budget by the number of graduates, equates to an unbelievable $312,500 per graduate. The state could afford to send all of its students to the best universities in the country for four years for what it costs to educate a student for one year in Alaska.

The high cost of education can be traced directly to the state's Constitution. The State of Alaska's Constitution outlines in three Articles with sixty four Sections the functions of the Legislative, Administrative and Judiciary branches of government. However, from a simple two Section reference in Article Seven titled, "Health, Education and Welfare," the university somehow has been able to assume for itself an exalted "sacred cow" status which in essence has made it a fourth branch of state government.

Some appointees to the Board of Regents over the years have been able to obtain fourth-branch-of-government status for the university system by capitalizing on the phrase in Section Two of Article Seven which, in addition to mandating the establishment of the university, grants it "body corporate" status. The checks and balances of power over this entity, as outlined in Section Three of this Article, are granted to the governor and a joint session of the Legislature. This power of oversight has not been utilized, through the years, in a judicious manner.

While the infamous reputation of the university seems to support the contention that a number of Board of Regents appointees have not been very good at setting policies that will promote quality education, they have been extremely skillful at empire building. One does not have to be very learned to understand when any corporation that is guaranteed hundreds of millions of dollars of non-taxable income yearly and is managed by a small group of people, that in time this corporation will "wheel" enormous power.

Thus, as the need arises, these people can utilize this power to serve as an effective barrier against challenges to its authority. The monster the citizens have allowed to be created has grown so strong that not many people are willing to challenge it because of security, social and political reasons.

Cost data on a recently constructed 94,000 square foot university building indicated that the building cost $269 a square foot to construct. This cost is more than double the cost ($121 per square foot) for constructing the largest privately owned building in downtown Anchorage.

Unfortunately, until enough citizens and political leaders develop the courage to challenge the university system in a fundamental way over its failure to promote equitable opportunity and generate a fair return on the citizens' substantial yearly investment, the citizens will continue to be faced with the fact that the university system represents a poor investment in an attempt to grow ivy on expensive buildings in Alaska.

To demonstrate the depth of the problem, the University of Alaska, has only two black faculty members who are on a tenure track, Dr. Elmer Haymon in the Department of Behavioral Science and Human Services.

Since relocating from Pittsburgh, Pennsylvania, Dr. Haymon has served in a number of leadership positions in the community to include president of the Greater Fairbanks Black Caucus, and the President of the Board of Directors of the Southside Community Center, and Chairman of the Fairbanks Minority Coalition.

Dr. Lisa Delpit is a member of the faculty in the Department of Education.

Alaska Pacific University, a small private liberal arts university located in Anchorage has Edwina Brown serving as University Controller. Dr. Velez Ramson formerly served as Dean of Students. Also, blacks have served on its Board of Trustees. This success record is due to the aggressive posture exhibited by the person who served as its president for nearly a decade, Dr. Glenn Olds. He is an internationally recognized scholar and humanitarian who retired as President Emeritus in 1987.

A number of blacks have held administrative positions in Alaska's public school systems. Far too often this opportunity only came after individual or collective struggles, not the natural consequence of being qualified. While some experiences have been positive, there are also a number of instances where their experiences in various educational capacities have been less than rewarding.

Dr. Thel Davis, after being a teacher in the Anchorage School District for many years, became the first black to serve as a principal in 1968 when she was put in charge of Fairview Elementary School. Since retiring from the District she has remained active in a number of volunteer capacities. Currently she directs a program to rehabilitate teenage shoplifters.

During an interview she laughingly stated, "When I have time, I just might write a book and call it The Games Public School Officials Play." As if someone might not understand why she would pick such a title for a book, she adds, "You know many of the games that public school administrators play is more related to petty organizational politics than it is to promoting quality education."

Bob Kelly was the first black to serve as a principal of a senior high school. He became a principal at Bartlett High School in the Fall of 1982. After serving in the capacity for four years, one year of which there were no classes held in his building due to a massive asbestos abatement project, he was reassigned to a position as Director of Migrant Education during his last year with the District, before retiring in June, 1987. General community sentiment was that his reassignment was the result of an orchestrated attack on his character by a District administrator and a vocal member of the community in which the school is located.

Dr. Lance Bowie is a product of the Anchorage School District who after graduation returned to teach in the District. He is now principal of Wendler Junior High School. Phyllis, his wife, is a teacher with the District.

After a number of promotions with the District to include positions as a principal of a junior high school and Director of Secondary Education, Dr. Carl LaMarr, was named as Assistant Superintendent for the Anchorage School District in 1985. His dissertation, The Relationship Among Principals' Leadership Behavior, Schools' Socio-economic Status, and Racial/ Ethnic Composition on Student Achievement in the Anchorage School District serves as a basis for some of the discussion to follow.

Sonya LaMarr's career in the Anchorage School District has paralleled that of her husband. She was appointed Principal of Government Hill Elementary School the Spring of in 1987. She is active in a number of groups. Currently she is serving as President of the Alaska Black Caucus.

The LaMarr's daughters, Carla and Cathie, who were educated in the Anchorage School System graduated from Howard University's Schools of Dentistry and Law respectively, in the summer of 1985.

Dr. Nancy Curtis, a person who put together the first organized work on blacks in Alaska in 1976, titled, Black Alaskans Salute America's Bicentennial (1776-1976), has maintained a running battle with the Anchorage School District since her dismissal as principal in the Spring of 1985. The black community is divided over the issue whether her reassignment was justified.

Other blacks who have or are serving as principals in the Anchorage School District include: Mary Boxx, Elliott Burgess, Mary Flynn, Rosa Foster, Tony Harduar, Bill Lester, Anna Seabrook, Clara Winbush, and Willis Williams.

Dr. Ken Burnley, out of the state of Michigan, was appointed Superintendent of Schools of the North Star Borough (Fairbanks) in Fall of 1981. In the Summer of 1987 he accepted the position of Superintendent of the School District in Colorado Springs, Colorado. There have been four blacks who have or are serving as principals in the Fairbanks school system: T. D. Dumas, Sandi Gamble, Darlene Haymon, and Yvonne Ryan.

Other persons around the state have made meaningful contributions to education to include Iola Banks in the Kenai School District and the legendary Charlie Mae Moore, Director of Teacher Certification for the State of Alaska's Department of Education.

In the public school system of Anchorage, primarily based on the fact that the housing patterns are racially mixed, the battles that have and continue to be waged over busing to achieve racial balance in schools in the contiguous states has not been an issue in Alaska. However, the issue that remains a concern as elsewhere in the nation is the performance of black students on standardized tests.

As a teacher, Pat Turner-Neverson, shared with persons participating in a workshop on education at the 17th Annual Congressional Black Caucus Legislative Weekend, in Washington, D. C. in 1987 "If we want our black children to improve their performance, then we as educators must provide them with a vision that reinforces the belief that achievement is not only possible, but it is an expectation."

Alaska's black students' performance on standardized tests is well above the national average for this population group. However, their performance remains below that of their majority counterparts. Possible explanations for this difference is presented as discussion and is not intended to add to the controversy researchers have engaged in for the past several decades.

Blacks as a percentage of the total student enrollment in the Anchorage School District has risen from 3.5 percent during the 1974/75 academic year to

6.7 percent for the 1984/85 academic year.[1] Total minority enrollment of the 40,000 student district is in excess of 22 percent.

The Alaska Black Leadership Conference's Community Based Educational Enrichment Program up until the Summer of 1987 had been a widely accepted approach to helping to raise the test scores of black students. In one of its annual reports to the Legislature its mission is clearly stated, "We of the Alaska Black Leadership Conference believe a continued effort is necessary to effectively raise achievement levels of minority students. Support is needed to transpose the decline of minority students' scores, and to help prevent the erosion of talent."

The rationale and philosophy underlying its mission bears further mention.

"Since each student lives in many worlds, the world of his primary family, his neighborhood, his peer group and his cultural heritage, he brings to school a unique set of customs, values and background experiences.

Most research indicates that attitudes are formed at a very early age and that many attitudes may be well established by the time a child completes the primary grades. This Community Based Education Program in part, is expected to help students to develop positive attitudes about themselves and about others.

It is based on the premise that if a person accepts himself/herself as having worth and dignity, he/she will not need to put down others in order to build up himself/herself. Moreover, it is based on the idea of helping children to see that similarities among people are those traits which make them members of the human family and differences among people are those characteristics which make each person special and unique.

It is hoped that through a multi-culturally based

TABLE XXII

Academic Year	Alaskan	American	Asian Pacific Islander	Filipino	Black	Hispanic	White	Other[a]	Total
1974-1975b	2,577		306		1,242	189	30,725	377	35,416
	7.30%		0.90%		3.50%	0.50%	86.80%	1.10%	100%
1975-1976b	2,548		481		1,668	350	33,394	355	38,796
	6.60%		1.20%		4.30%	0.90%	86.10%	0.90%	100%
1976-1977b	2,548		667		1,761	428	32,790	187	38,381
	6.60%		1.70%		4.60%	1.10%	85.40%	0.50%	100%
1977-1978b	2,588	200	678	174	1,907	550	32,250		38,347
	6.70%	0.50%	1.80%	0.40%	5.00%	1.40%	84.10%		100%
1978-1979b	2,529	235	752	197	2,105	650	30,987		37,455
	6.80%	0.60%	2.00%	0.50%	5.60%	1.70%	82.70%		100%
1979-1980b	2,535	260	792	211	2,172	795	29,105		35,870
	7.10%	0.70%	2.20%	0.60%	6.10%	1.90%	81.40%		100%
1981-1982c	2489	313	851	209	2259	793	28699		35,613
	6.90%	1.00%	2.40%	0.70%	6.60%	2.20%	80.60%		100%
1982-1983d	2412	394	1041	265	2522	838	30948		38,420
	6.30%	1.00%	2.70%	0.70%	6.60%	2.20%	80.60%		100%
1983-1984e	2,570	416	1,145	323	2,615	938	32,443	2	40,452
	6.40%	1.00%	2.80%	0.80%	6.50%	2.30%	80.20%		100%
1984-1985f	2,593	412	1,335	384	2,815	1,027	33,372		41,938
	6.20%	1.00%	3.20%	0.90%	6.70%	2.40%	79.60%		100%

TABLE XXII (Page 200)
ETHNIC COMPOSITION OF THE ANCHORAGE SCHOOL DISTRICT
1974-75 THROUGH 1984-85

a. This category was called "Unknown" in school year 1977-78.
b. Membership figures given are based on end of the year active enrollment.
c. Membership as of March 11, 1982.
d. Membership as of September 14, 1982.
e. Membership as of October 4, 1983.
f. Membership as of February 1, 1985.

Note: The categories Alaskan Native and American Indian were combined before 1977. The Filipino category was included with Asia-Pacific Islander until 1977.

curriculum children will begin to see that differences are not negative, but rather, that they are positive and add interest and richness to life. This philosophy can help children see that one of the beauties of the United States is that it is a composite of many people whose cultures have blended to create a culture which is richer than any single culture from which it is drawn.

Instructions in the area of multi-cultural education also requires the teacher to project a balance. For many years individual and cultural differences were brushed aside with the oversimplification that "we are all really alike." This was often referred to as the 'Melting Pot' ideology.

The United States is a land of diversity whose quality of character springs from the creativity, the toil, and the indulgence of individuals of all races and cultures. It is important, therefore, that every individual understand and appreciate the similarities and differences subsisting in all people of this country who contributed to America's heritage. We are all charged with a inescapable task; to help each child develop positive self concepts."

The Conference's noble goals, as well as its aspirations, have suffered a serious blow as a result of some insensitive budget action taken by the Cowper Administration in June of 1987. When pressed for an explanation by community leaders as to why funding for the program had been eliminated, the response from staff was that the "Governor was not interested in funding Sheffield's pet programs." For the historical record the program was first funded under the Hammond Administration and only continued under the Sheffield Administration. This action by the Cowper Administration has so alienated the black community, it's doubtful that Governor Cowper will ever again enjoy the broad based support he received for his initial campaign.

The Conference effects and the commitment pledged to the community by the immediate past Superintendent of Schools, Dr. E. E. (Gene) Davis, who retired from the District in June, 1987, has resulted in blacks raising their performance levels from the 41 percentile in 1982 to the 46 percentile in 1986[2].

Dr. William Coats, whose previous experience include stints as Superintendent of two districts in Michigan, and a professorship at the University of Michigan, was appointed Superintendent of the Anchorage School District in May, 1987. The concepts he has shared with community groups, and his publicly stated expectations for administrators and teachers gives confidence for continued improvement in the performance of all students on standardized tests. His early outreach efforts, pronouncements and the fact he comes highly recommended by many nationally known educators, as well as black leaders in the areas he previously held positions, seem to support a hope for better days ahead. Just before this book went to press, he appointed Dr. Gene Thompson as Deputy Superintendent for Instruction, a person who shares his views for improving academic achievement. Also, he is in the process of identifying a person to pull together the functions of community relations, bilingual, and multicultural education. The lack of emphasis these programs have received in the past has been a source of concern for minority communities for a number of years.

A eview of the data of the overall performance of blacks' on standardized tests reveal that the disparity in test scores is considerably less than the national average between blacks and whites. Performance of SAT and ACT tests for black students taking these exams in Alaska is measurable higher than the performance of their counterparts in the contiguous states.

TABLE XXIII
AVERAGE NORMAL CURVE EQUIVALENT SCORES AND CORRESPONDING PERCENTILE RANK SCORES (1984-85 NORM EQUIVALENTS)
ITBS AND TAP COMPOSITES COMBINED ACROSS GRADE LEVELS 1982 THROUGH 1986

RACIAL/ETHNIC GROUP	DATA TYPE	1982	1983	1984	1985	1986
Alaskan	Mean NCE	42.2	43.2	44.9	45.6	47.5
Natives	Percentile	36	37	40	42	45
	Number Tested	2,047	1,938	1,953	1,949	1,887
American	Mean NCE	45.6	47.3	48.3	49	52
Indians	Percentile	42	45	47	48	54
	Number Tested	313	331	363	325	275
Asians	Mean NCE	51.4	51.3	53.4	54.7	56.5
	Percentile	53	52	56	59	62
	Number Tested	753	884	974	1,058	1,166
Blacks	Mean NCE	40.9	41	42.9	43	45.7
	Percentile	33	33	37	37	42
	Number Tested	2,006	2,120	2,120	2,260	2,356
Filipinos	Mean NCE	48.4	48.2	48.8	49.8	50.7
	Percentile	47	47	48	50	51
	Number Tested	203	238	274	305	336
Hispanics	Mean NCE	44.8	44.7	46.7	46.9	49.1
	Percentile	40	40	44	44	48
	Number Tested	705	718	728	824	841
Whites	Mean NCE	54.5	54.5	56.4	57	59
	Percentile	58	58	62	63	67
	Number Tested	26,083	26,929	27,140	27,991	26,834
All Students	Mean NCE	52.5	52.6	54.4	55	56.9
	Percentile	55	55	58	59	63
	Number Tested	32,110	33,158	33,552	34,712	33,695

Congressman Walter Fauntroy, District of Columbia, with Dr. Carl LaMarr at a Jesse Jackson for President reception held during the Congressman's visit to Alaska in 1984.

TABLE XXIV

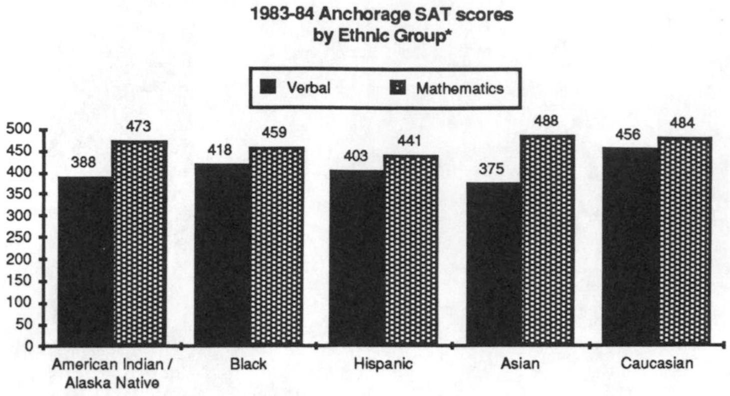
1983-84 Anchorage SAT scores
by Ethnic Group*
Verbal
Mathematics
500
450
400
350
300
250
200
150
100
50
0
388
473
418
459
403
441
375
488
456
484
American Indian / Alaska Native
Black
Hispanic
Asian
Caucasian

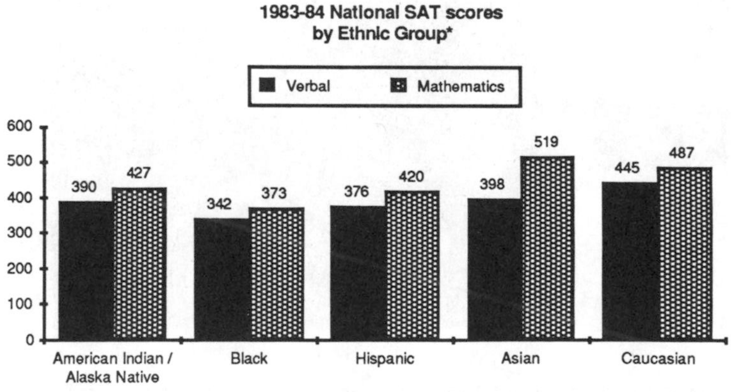
1983-84 National SAT scores
by Ethnic Group*
Verbal
Mathematics
600
500
400
300
200
100
0
390
427
342
373
376
420
398
519
445
487
American Indian / Alaska Native
Black
Hispanic
Asian
Caucasian

TABLE XXV

1983-84 Anchorage ACT scores
by Ethnic Group*
Special Report by ACT

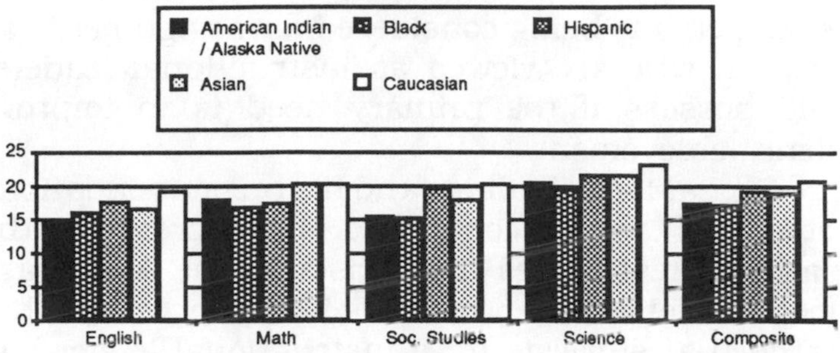

1983-84 National ACT scores
by Ethnic Group*
Special Report by ACT

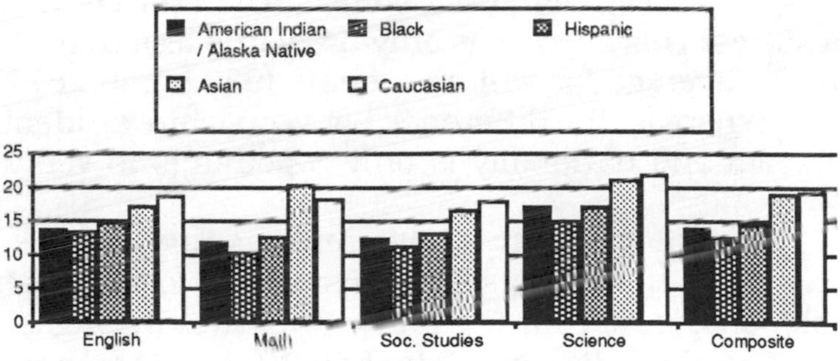

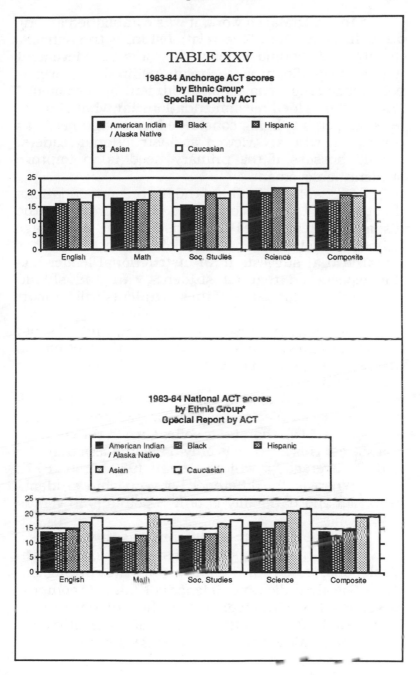

In Dr. LaMarr's work, it was established among other findings that, "the relationship of the schools' racial/ethnic compositions with student achievement is not as significant as the relationship of the principals' leadership behavior with student achievement." The work provided recommendations for what characteristics persons being considered for assignments as principals, who are viewed as instructional leaders, should possess if the primary need is to improve student achievement.

Dr. LaMarr's findings and his recommendations if acted upon, would contribute to a decrease in the disparity of test scores that exists in the Anchorage School District. Further, his work is supported by other research that suggests if an instructional leader has the expectation that all students can and should achieve the performance of these students will support the expectation.

However, his research does not, and was not intended to provide an explanation for the fact blacks in Alaska out perform their colleagues elsewhere in the United States.

On the SAT test the combined verbal and mathematics score for blacks in Alaska is 162 points higher (877 versus 715)[3] than their colleagues in the contiguous states. This average is only 54 points less than the national average for white students (932 versus 877).

Whereas, the difference between white students in Alaska and nationally is only 8 points (940 versus 932).

A similar margin of difference is noted on performance on the ACT test. The test scores for blacks in Alaska on the ACT for the four composites of English, Math, Social Studies and Science is 17.3. This composite score is 4.6 points higher than the national average for blacks (17.3 versus 12.7).[4] For whites the difference is less than half of that for blacks (21.0 versus 19.3).

Without any supporting empirical justification, the following environmental conditions are offered as possible explanations. The levels of income and education of blacks living in Alaska is considerably higher than that of our counterparts in the other states.

Nationally only two in every hundred black families have incomes in excess of $50,000 a year. In Alaska one in every nine families have income in excess of $50,000.[5] The figure is nearly twice the national average of whites which is one in twenty.

Nationally, just over 50 percent of blacks have a high school education. In Alaska 83 percent of the blacks have a high school or beyond education.

This observation should be the basis for more quantitative research to determine to what extent family income and education levels of black parents in Alaska have on the academic performance on standardized tests by their children.

Also, the elimination of corporal punishment because some parents believed teachers were abusing their children may have had an impact on achievement. If teachers are unable to discipline students, their ability to impact knowledge will suffer. Our inability to accept this fact has placed some of us in the position where we must concoct outlandish rationales and excuses in an attempt to explain some of our student's undisciplined behavior and sub-par performance.

Home environments should reinforce the benefits to be derived from discipline with the hope such reinforcement will have a carry-over effect to school environments.

Any objective analysis will most assuredly reveal that discipline is germane to all educational achievement. Historically, education has been one of the keys to black progress in America.

1. See Table XXII.
2. See Table XXIII.
3. See Table XXIV.
4. See Table XXV.
5. See Table XI, Chapter VIII.

CHAPTER XII
CHALLENGES AND OPPORTUNITIES OF THE NEXT CENTURY

The main challenges facing blacks in Alaska during the remainder of this century, and well into the next, are searching for ways to combat racism, and overcoming the obstacles it places to political and economic empowerment.

As elsewhere, improving race relations has not been on the Alaskan agenda of priorities for a number of years. Because of this fact, could one conclude that our nation and state have moved too far to the right on views about race? Correspondingly, creating the climate for a rise in racism. In 1986 and early 1987 there were a number of nationally reported incidents relating to race that took place in the states of Georgia, Florida and New York.

In order to attempt to access what the future holds for racism and prejudice in Alaska, one must understand the motives of the persons who are defining the terms, as well as being able to distinguish the difference between racism and prejudice.

If we accept the fact that the publicized incidences of racism in our society being perpetrated by individuals, groups, and institutions are at alarming levels for a civilized and democratic society, we must also conclude it is a form of ignorance that has been desegregated in America.

While it is difficult to admit, we as blacks often aid and abet the brand of racism being practiced by some members of the majority culture. The reasons are our inability to discern when statements are racially motivated, and our mistaken belief that the powers that be in our society are interested in integrating unequals (people who do not exercise their power). The inability to discern intent does not relate to anyone needing to confront, agonize or analyze the reasons individuals choose to use derogatory terms to deny another person's existence because of their need to mask inadequacies. As will be discussed later, the major problem for blacks is our inability to make the call on racism in a political context.

This difficulty merely reflects the changes in our society. Since it is no longer acceptable to lynch undesirable or "uppity" blacks in an overt manner, racism has had to be institutionalized so that the now symbolic practice of public hangings could be continued in a covert manner.

With predictable regularity, the Justice System goes after visual blacks. If one doubts this assertion, all one needs to recall is how the FBI constantly attempted to discredit Dr. Martin Luther King Jr. in the mid-sixties or the attacks on high profile political organizers in the eighties such as Arnold Pinkney, who was the brains behind the Jesse Jackson for President candidacy in 1984. In a nationally publicized case Mr. Pickney, who is a business civic leader, and insurance broker in Cleveland, Ohio, was charged with using his political office (Cuyahoga County Commissioner) for personal gain. The court records show the alleged gain totaled $263. Yet, the system was willing to spend hundreds of thousands of dollars to take the matter to trial, all but one of the counts were dismissed. He paid a small fine and was placed on probation.

When black leaders are forced to defend themselves against public hangings supported by institutional racism often funded with public money, it accomplishes three objectives for racists. Fortunately this group remains the true minority in our nation.

It creates public doubt about the leaders true motives, damages their creditability with the masses, and it makes it more difficult to organize blacks into a political power.

Compounding the problem all too often the word racism and prejudice are used interchangeably. Realizing the difference between prejudice and racism is as difficult as attempting to define the difference between a predicament and a problem.

As such it is often easier to cite examples than to provide definitions. At the end of 1986 Alaska was faced with predicament of declining oil revenues. The incredible problem that exists is that some state legislators are suggesting as a solution increasing taxation of an industry that is already supplying 85 percent of the state's revenue.

Another predicament we are faced with in Alaska is racism. The problem is that a number of people are attempting to define racism as merely the existence of prejudicial attitudes.

A necessary first sign in addressing the predicament and eliminating the problem is for persons who have access to public forums to stop compounding the problem by interchanging the use of the words prejudice and racism.

In Alaska, as like other regions in our nation, we all are guilty of exhibiting some basic prejudicial attitudes. In a number of instances these attitudes are not race specific. On the other hand, racism is the practice whereby a group of people use a system of laws, political, economic and military power or numerical dominance to deny equal access, maintain a state of subservience, imprison or enslave another group of people solely on the basis of race.

Exercising political power is a necessary first step for obtaining economic power. As noted in Chapter V, at the end of 1987 blacks held only five of the 560 public offices in Alaska.[1] In state government, under Governor Steve Cowper's Administration, of the 900 plus positions that serve at the pleasure of the Governor only four were filled by blacks as the first quarter of 1987 expired. Three of the positions were holdovers from the previous administration. This statistic is quite distressing in that he actively campaigned and received substantial volunteer, monetary, and voting support for his successful candidacy in 1986 from the black community. While this realization is distressing, it illustrates, like the limited number of elected black officials, the depth of the problem that must be overcome to gain political strength.

In voting what we thought were our interests in the 1986 gubernatorial election, we were again betrayed. However, a lone betrayal will not deter us from the plan to vote our self interests. When we fail to vote our interests, this allows one of the major parties in the state to take us for granted and the other to write us off and spend its time organizing other constituency groups to counter blacks' effectiveness. Also, we must rid ourselves of the mistaken belief that people in power will respect and accept us if they like us. All this belief does is to allow persons in power to treat us with contempt or more benignly in patronizing ways.

Public capital construction in Alaska has provided futile ground in which to plant the seeds of racism.

Most people who have knowledge of the public construction industry in Alaska are familiar with the terms "preferences" and "quotas."

The masses who are not generally familiar with the industry are often misled by persons who have industry-related knowledge of these terms.

On one hand, they support the "motherhood" issue of giving five percent preference to Alaska firms bidding on state contracts and on the other hand they incite people by giving them incomplete and misleading information that quotas are un-American. The special interests that control the construction industry exhibit no remorse that their positions are grossly inconsistent. When someone or some entity is assigned a fixed percentage based on some state criterion so that they might pursue an economic opportunity utilizing the public wealth, whether it is called by the politically and socially acceptable term "preference," or the racially divisive term "quota," it's the same thing.

The term quota has been the rallying cry used by persons who control the public construction industry to mis-focus attention and sustain racial resentment between "white have nots and black never hads."

The prime perception they have created in the people's minds is that quotas sanctioned by law relating to public construction projects are unconstitutional. They accomplish this by confusing the public over the difference between two rulings handed down by the U. S. Supreme Court.

While the U. S. Supreme Court stuck down as unconstitutional the quota system for admission to a medical school in California (Bakey Decision), the court upheld the constitutionality of the 10 percent quota contained in the Public Works Employment Act of 1977 in its Fullilove v. Klugtznick decision. The 1980 ruling stated, "The interest in facilitating and encouraging the participation by minority business enterprises in the economy is unquestionably legitimate. Any barrier to such entry and growth - whether grounded in the law or in irrational prejudice - should be vigorously and thoroughly removed. Equality of economic opportunity is a goal of no less importance than quality of employment opportunity."

The people controlling the public construction industry know these facts, yet they continue to promote resentment by capitalizing on the ignorance of the general public to the facts. They would have you believe that the American way of life is under siege by blacks with a "government handout" mentality and that it's their duty to fight to preserve America's values.

In Alaska during the fiscal years between July, 1981 - July, 1983 more than $1.1 billion of capital-projects money was appropriated and hundreds of prime and subcontracts were issued by the state and blacks received only seven subcontracts totaling less than three tenths of 1 percent of the public wealth.

One key to building political power in Alaska will depend on how effective we are in organizing coalitions. Such an approach will allow the members of the coalition to leverage their influence of their numbers. This is especially critical in Alaska because of historically close elections. The gubernatorial primary in 1978 and 1982 were decided by 98 and 238 votes respectively.

As of the end of 1986 the black population in Alaska was estimated to be 21,300 people. If the persons of voting age in this population coalesced with other interest groups and given the history of close elections, such a coalition could have a significant impact on Alaskan politics.

A surface appreciation for coalition building could lead one to conclude that like the "lower 48" coalitions could be formed between blacks, other minorities and labor unions. Formulation of such an alliance is not as natural as it would be in the contiguous states. The prime reasons being the lack of black and Native interaction, and the fact those industries which have been unionized in large numbers in the contiguous states are not in evidence in Alaska.

The limited social, and non-existence of political interaction between black and Natives has resulted in attitudes being formed that range from benign concern or perplexity to borderline resentment. While there has been a documented presence of blacks in Alaska for over a hundred years, it appears the current attitudes were formed within the past two decades.

Blacks who have a benign concern seem to struggle with their emotions when they perceive Native leaders are plotting an isolationist, go-it-alone strategy for their people. Blacks' experience seems to support the contention that the road to progress in this society is often made easier by coalition building.

A review of the census data would seem to support a concerned people's attitude that an isolationist posture coupled with a continued rural lifestyle, if not stemmed, will by the mid 21st century relegate Natives to a de facto reservation existence. Less than two generations ago (1930 census) Natives comprised 50 percent of Alaska's population; today their percentage is around 17 percent of which two-thirds maintain a rural lifestyle. It is interesting to note during the same period, blacks' percentages have grown to where they represent the largest minority group in Alaska's two largest cities.

To further support their concern, blacks point out the fact that while our American society continues to grow more humane and pluralistic in its cultural diversity, it still possesses a latent propensity to inflict inhumane treatment on targeted sub-groups. Especially when these groups are culturally, socially and geographically isolated. If one doubts this premise, the Japanese-American experience just four decades ago should serve as a vivid reminder.

Blacks who harbor feelings of resentment perceive Natives to be the direct beneficiaries of the struggles waged by blacks, whites, Hispanic and Asian Americans during the fifties and sixties without having to pay any dues.

Further, blacks realize many of the inherently good qualities that a representative democracy possesses can and often are manipulated or even negated by a few skillful, elected and major corporate politicians to serve their desired ends.

With this knowledge, people with little or no concern are amused to see the 20th century version of the "give them fire water and negotiate with trinkets game being run." Some blacks appear to relish in this fact and know the well intended piece of social legislation called the Native Claims Settlement Act, passed by Congress in 1971, with its heavy political overtones, is doomed for economic failure. However they question why they were not counseled or invited to share in some of the "up front" benefits derived from the passage of the act.

The percentage split on the perceptions held by Alaska closely approximates the split that always is associated with controversial issues. Twenty percent truly understand the issue, and therefore, support it, 20 percent have no understanding of the issue, therefore, oppose it, and 60 percent have no opinion but desire more information so they may form an opinion.

It is the latter percentage group, not only as it relates to black and Native relations, but obviously also the majority culture's attitude that must shift to the side of better understanding if coalitions are to be built.

Coalition building with unions in Alaska presents a number of obstacles, the decline in unionism notwithstanding.

Nationally, labor statistics indicate that in 1970 there were 78.5 million Americans employed and the unemployment rate was 4.9 percent. Union workers totaled 20.7 million, or 26.4 percent of the total work-force.

Stated another way, approximately one of every four workers in 1970 was a member of organized labor.

Statistics gathered at the end of 1979 revealed that nearly 100 million Americans were employed and the unemployment rate was 7.1 percent. Organized labor represented 22 million workers or 22 percent of the work-force, representing a drop of 4.4. percentage points in 10 years. Now approximately one of five workers is a union member.

The difference might not seem to be significant. However, when viewed from the perspective that during the last decade nearly 22.5 million new jobs were created and of this number fewer than 2 million of these workers became members of unions, then the situation is much more critical.

Fewer than one of every 10 new workers over the last decade joined unions. Understanding the historical working conditions that existed in this country that gave rise to the need for workers to organize, one would surely be concerned as to what are the factors that contributed to this precipitous decline in unionism?

Union bosses would probably provide the rationalization that during the same period of time employment in the manufacturing industry, which is heavily unionized, as a percentage of the total jobs available, dropped an identical 4.4 percent. They would, therefore, say unionism is not in decline but merely reflects the current employment conditions.

While such a rationalization provides a "happy face" to mask the obvious erosion of the strength of unions, it does nothing to alleviate the condition.

Unionism in this country will continue to decline for reasons unrelated to our country shifting from an industrial to technological base of employment.

The reasons organized labor as a force in the work-place will continue to suffer setbacks are because of its leadership's constant backing of often unimaginative political office seekers, the failure of this same leadership to understand the world as a marketplace and the resulting unrealistic representations to the rank and file.

In the skilled construction crafts, especially here in Alaska, instances of favoritism at the expense of minorities and females have detracted from organizing efforts.

Even in the few construction unions in which minorities and females hold memberships, there are indications that members are not dispatched in an equitable manner. The most repugnant behavior by union members was exhibited by the pipewelders from Oklahoma. Their refusal to work with minorities and females during the construction of the oil pipeline in the seventies was infamous. There was an incident on a camp bus where they brutalized a minority member of Teamsters Local 959. This behavior and employment practices served as a basis for a finding against the union for its discriminatory acts. The order mandated that in future employment situations they provide equitable treatment for workers.

While the obstacles to coalition building between blacks, Natives and unions in Alaska are formidable, it would appear its in our respective self interests to search for ways to foster such a coalition as a way of promoting political power.

For blacks to gain an equitable economic threshold in Alaska, we will need to assess the marketplace for opportunities, and utilize our political base to take advantage of both employment and entrepreneurial opportunities.

To take advantage of employment opportunities, one must first understand what is contributing to current unemployment in our country and state.

There is an ever expanding core group of unemployable, yet often willing, workers in our society. The condition of high unemployment is the result of a number of factors that are confluent at this point in our history and can not be rationalized away by laying the blame at the doorstep of the current occupant in the White House.

The world as a marketplace, antedated industrial plants, advancing technology, the constant struggle for control over the skilled American workforce and mis-education are factors in the unemployment equation of far greater significance than presidential policies.

It's a cruel hoax to play on the American people by politically motivated critics of present supply side economic policy to suggest that a cosmetic change in economic policy will eradicate unemployment.

Granted, certain artificially induced public incentives could be instituted that would moderate the unemployment figures. However, such influences would be short-lived and would not impact the fundamental root causes contributing to unemployment.

An important factor in our current high unemployment picture is the relative position of the U. S. with other industrialized nations in regards to the implementation of new technology. The U. S. was one of the first countries to employ industrialized technology by constructing modern factories which utilized advanced production techniques at the turn of the century. Our current standard of living to a great extent was built on the efficiency of our steel, transportation and manufacturing industries none which are in evidence in Alaska.

We are currently faced with a new revolution. This time it is technical rather than industrial. While we were first to embrace the industrial revolution, we have lagged behind in entering the technicalogical revolution. To be sure, the U. S. still leads the world in technical achievements. However, a few countries are far ahead of us in putting these advancements to practical uses. While we continue to struggle with labor intensive industrial techniques, they are building new factories and manufacturing facilities employing state of the art "robotics," communications, and advanced technologies. Additionally, with the sum of human knowledge doubling every 20 to 30 years, it is unrealistic to expect that a 12 year public education system instituted approximately a hundred years ago can equip our youth with the skills necessary to deal with the consequences of the "information explosion" without some fundamental restructuring.

Private industry leaders must communicate to educators what skills will be needed to take advantage of future opportunities. Higher education missions should be redefined. Our community colleges could serve as the vehicle to equip our core group of unemployable with skills that will allow them to move in new areas of opportunity as well as developing programs to utilize and service new technology. Our universities can continue to facilitate theoretical learning and research.

Understanding conditions, and anticipating needs should allow Alaskans in general and blacks in particular to make gains commensurate with the growth of Alaska.

One of the major avenues for economic improvement, private use of and, unlike other states, will for the foreseeable future remain virtually non-existent in Alaska.

The Alaska Land Preservation Act of 1980,

popularly referred to as the D-2 Lands Act, locked up Alaska's land to any meaningful development. Under the provision of the Act the Federal Government maintained ownership of 217.7 million acres or nearly 59.2 percent of all of Alaska's land. The state was entitled to select 104.8 million acres or 28.5 percent, and the 13 Native Corporations, which were established under the Native Claims Act of 1971, are entitled to 43.7 million acres or approximately 11.8 percent. This leaves only 1.5 million acres available for private ownership.

When acreage already in private residential ownership is discounted from the 1.5 million acres, the opportunity for the development of significant independent commercial enterprises is not available. Further the cost of doing business in an isolated region of the world which has only limited transportation networks will essentially remain cost prohibitive to all but a few multi-national firms.

Economic opportunities for individuals, small investment groups, and businesses will be confined to the prudent buying and selling of limited acreage in urban areas.

Such an economic undertaking can be either pursued on an individual basis, as currently in evidence, and on a collective development basis. Development and venture capital sources are well established. However, an approach to capital formation that has to date not been pursued, which was originally proposed by Andonia Harrison during her second term as Anchorage Branch, NAACP President, was for blacks to pool their Alaska Permanent Fund dividend checks.[2]

In 1987 each man, woman and child in Alaska will receive a check from the state of Alaska in the amount of $718. Each year the check received by the citizens of Alaska has increased in value. Translated this will mean that the approximately 22,000 blacks living in Alaska during 1987, will receive a total of 15.8

million dollars, in a direct payment from the state.

If only 10 percent of this population invested in a fund for development, a total of 1.58 million dollars annually would be available for investment at no direct cost or liability to the participants.

If this amount was invested annually at 10 percent as of January 1, 1988, by the end of this century the fund would be worth over 37 million dollars.

Additionally, opportunities will continue to exist in the delivery of services to the population by professionals. Table XXVII categorizes, by professions, blacks that were providing professional services at the end of 1986.

William Browner, his wife, Pat and their children, established their home in Anchorage in 1978 when he was discharged from the Air Force. Just a few short years later, he is unable to accommodate all the referrals and requests for his pediatric services.

Attorney Rex Butler, after a short stint with the State of Alaska's Attorney General's Office, opened up a private practice. A number of cases he has tried have received state-wide attention. However, his active practice has not prevented him from advocating for social change. He challenged the powers that be for much of 1986 for their failure to resolve the controversy surrounding the naming of a public facility in tribute to Dr. Martin Luther King, Jr.

Further, his warning about the existence of undetected levels of racism as personified by the controversy went unheeded. When the Anchorage Municipal Assembly finally voted to name a yet to be completed performing arts center, that has experienced multi-million dollar cost overruns, in honor of King, a petition was circulated by a former Assemblyman, Don Smith, to have the honor rescinded. He was able to gain the necessary signatures to have the issue place before the voters as a ballot issue. The voters of Anchorage on October 6, 1987 voted by a margin of three to one to rescind the Assembly's action in naming the center after Dr. King. The situation was reported nationally in the October 23, 1987 edition of the New York Times in a column by Daily News reporter, Hal Spencer, and the October 26, 1987 issue of Jet Magazine. The magazine story dealt with the situation from the perspective that Anchorage's bid to host the 1994 Winter Olympics may have been damaged with Third World Nations. These nations will be among those of the International Olympic Committee that will be voting for a city among the six vying to host the 1994 Winter Olympics in September 1988. Along with Rex Butler community activist, Charles Robinson, raised this issue as a possibility early in 1987.

Winston Henderson, out of Dallas, Texas has maintained an independent architectural practice for much of the decade of the eighties. His design of the First CME Church at the corner of 36th/McInnes has been nominated for several outstanding design awards by professional societies.

Because of the ethnic diversity of Alaska, the success of these gentlemen's respective professional practices is dependent on their ability to market and provide quality service to an ethnically diverse clientele.

As outlined in Chapter XI blacks' education levels are comparable to that of their majority counterparts. This fact should allow us to compete for administrative positions in both the public and private sectors. Opportunities with the public school systems in Alaska should continue to exist well into the next century. National statistics substantiate the fact that Alaskan teachers are the highest paid in the nation. In 1986 the average annual salary topped $41,000.

While there are encouraging signs, the ability to bring about change in Alaska must not be underestimated by blacks. Bringing about change in a state that oftentimes takes foolish pride in promoting isolationism can be an extremely laborious and a frustrating experience. A classic example exists in this regard. Bob Uchitel, a prominent civic and business leader of the early eighties, became so disenchanted with the lack of vision possessed by a host of political leaders that he took out a full page newspaper ad announcing that he would no longer be a source for campaign contributions for spineless and unimaginative politicians. The source of his frustration was that to many public officials were willing to promote isolationism at the expense of the state's destiny. Politicians were opposed to Uchitel's vision that Alaska celebrate its 25th Anniversary as a state back in 1984 utilizing the vehicle of a World's Fair to improve and promote the state's image as a place where cross-cultural understanding and racial tolerance are the norms.

If at least one copy of this book remains in existence in the year 2087, it would prove to be an interesting exercise if someone assessed whether blacks met the challenges and enjoyed what Alaska presented to them a hundred years earlier near the end of the 20th century.

1. The number of public offices in Alaska that require a Conflict of Interest statement to be filed with the Public Offices Commission.
2. The Alaska Permanent Fund is a savings account restricted as to usage, which belongs to all the people of Alaska. It was created by public referendum in 1976. The fund utilizes 25 percent of the state's income derived from energy and mineral sources. A portion of the interest earnings from the fund is paid directly to the residents of Alaska.

Attorney Rex Butler

Winston H. Henderson, A.I.A.

TABLE XVII
BLACK PROFESSIONALS

PROFESSION	NUMBER
Ph. D.'s	50[1]
Medical Doctors	6
Dentists	1
Attorneys	9[2]
Architects	1[2]
Engineers	2[2]

1. Estimated.
2. Actual number of persons holding degrees in these professions are higher than listed. However, these persons have not obtained or sought licensing in Alaska.

TABLES

PHOTO CREDITS

Danny Martin, Anchorage Daily News
Fran Durner, Anchorage Daily News
Hegg Collection
Office of Military History, U. S. Navy
University of Washington Archives

BIBLIOGRAPHY

Alaska Felony Sentences: 1984, Alaska Judicial Council, March, 1987.
Alaska State Constitution
Alaska State Statutes

A report on the Department of Transportation and Public Facilities Civil Rights Office Affirmative Action Employment and Contracting, State of Alaska, Budget and Audit Committee, April 15, 1986.

Congressional Record, October 10, 1979.

Interim Report of the Alaska Judicial Council on Findings Apparent Racial, Disparity in Sentencing, Alaska Judicial Council, October, 1979.

Task Force on Minority Enterprise of the Subcommittee on General Oversight and Minority Enterprise of the Committee on Small Business, House of Representatives, 96th Congress, Second Session, Anchorage, Alaska, July 16, 17, 1980.

"Report on the Shooting Death of Phillip Moore," State of Alaska, Departments of Public Safety and Law, June 18, 1979.

Ulysses Lee, "The Employment of Negro Troops," Office of Military History

U. S. Census, 1980.

INDEX

A

B

C